SCEPTICAL CHRISTIANITY

of related interest

The Forgiveness Project
Stories for a Vengeful Age
Marina Cantacuzino
Forewords by Archbishop Emeritus Desmond Tutu and Alexander McCall Smith
ISBN 978 1 84905 566 6 [Hardback]
ISBN 978 1 78592 000 4 [Paperback]
eISBN 978 1 78450 006 1

Towards Better Disagreement
Religion and Atheism in Dialogue
Paul Hedges
ISBN 978 1 78592 057 8
eISBN 978 1 78450 316 1

Re-enchanting the Activist
A Spirituality of Social Change
Keith Hebden
ISBN 978 1 78592 041 7
eISBN 978 1 78450 295 9

SCEPTICAL CHRISTIANITY

Exploring Credible Belief

Robert Reiss

Jessica Kingsley *Publishers*
London and Philadelphia

First published in 2016
by Jessica Kingsley Publishers
73 Collier Street
London N1 9BE, UK
and
400 Market Street, Suite 400
Philadelphia, PA 19106, USA

www.jkp.com

Front cover image source: iStockphoto®.

Library of Congress Cataloging in Publication Data
Names: Reiss, Robert (Canon Emeritus of Westminster Abbey)
Title: Sceptical Christianity : exploring credible belief / Robert Reiss.
Description: Philadelphia : Jessica Kingsley Publishers, 2016.
Identifiers: LCCN 2016004137 | ISBN 9781785920622 (alk. paper)
Subjects: LCSH: Apologetics. | Skepticism.
Classification: LCC BT1103 .R45 2016 | DDC 239--dc23 LC
record available at https://lccn.loc.gov/2016004137

British Library Cataloguing in Publication Data
A CIP catalogue record for this book is available from the British Library

ISBN 978 1 78592 062 2
eISBN 978 1 78450 318 5

Printed and bound in the United States

For my daughter, Anya

Contents

Acknowledgements

Any book outlining what someone believes will owe a vast amount to other people. This is no exception. Former teachers, authors, lecturers, parishioners and even filmmakers have influenced me for the more than 50 years since I started thinking carefully about theology, as have countless conversations with friends and colleagues. Even those I remember would be a long list, but there were many other conversations which no doubt influenced me, but with whom I cannot now remember.

Since making the decision to write this book I have tried out parts or, in two cases, all on other people; their comments have been immensely helpful. In alphabetical order I am particularly grateful to Robert Cotton, Jeremy Davies, Helen Freeman, Robert Gage, Anthony and Rosemary Hawley, Oliver Letwin, Jennifer Schwalbenberg and Richard and Clare Staughton. Even, or maybe especially, when they have disagreed with me, I have found their comments thought-provoking and illuminating. I must record my thanks to them all, although of course I take full personal responsibility for my conclusions.

I should also thank my atheist wife, Dixie Nichols, who advocated my writing this book on the grounds that 'after all that's what all your sermons are always about'. She also proved a merciless critic, always overstating her argument, but rather often actually being right.

My daughter, Anya, who is an author in a very different field, probably disagrees with her father on all manner of things. I have dedicated this book to her. At least she will now have the chance to know what I do and do not believe. I do not expect her fully to agree!

Preface

Why I wrote this book

I have tried to set down what I do – and do not – believe. That might seem a strange thing for a clergyman to do. After all, clergy surely have an obligation to speak for orthodox Christian Faith.

But what exactly constitutes orthodox Christian Faith? Not only do clergy disagree with each other about practical moral issues such as gay marriage, or the use of armed force, but also about core Christian beliefs such as the nature of God, or what happens to us after death. Worse, these beliefs do not just vary between individuals; they may change within each individual over time.

In the nearly 50 years since my ordination, I have changed my mind on all sorts of aspects of my Christian belief – sometimes because a particular experience has pushed me to think more deeply, but more often as a result of the wider intellectual world: a lecture, a book, a film.

Speaking broadly, my acceptance of the traditional tenets of Christianity has, over the years, evolved to a more sceptical position. In part, that reflects a sea change in the present intellectual climate, which has actually become much more sceptical. Of course, there is a kind of scepticism that owes more to cynicism than anything else; I do not want to be part of that.

But I do feel a moral responsibility to examine the evidence for different aspects of my belief.

I have come to think that the Church of England is not currently engaged as deeply as it might be with this contemporary scepticism. Since David Jenkins was Bishop of Durham, if I look for examples of episcopal engagement with such matters the stable looks pretty bare – no doubt because many of the bishops, for understandable reasons, are reluctant to upset the more traditional members of their dioceses. They also seem to be more concerned with the management of the Church, and with questions of form rather than content. Fresh Expressions of the Church are welcomed without examining what is being expressed and whether it is true. Of course, some bishops simply defend traditional belief, but that is not the sympathetic engagement with scepticism I am talking about. For me, the silence of all but a very few bishops is deafening, and I wonder how much it has contributed to the increasing marginalising of Christian belief. I also fear that too many current academic theologians are so engaged in an internal conversation with themselves that they fail to write for a wider sceptical world.

It has not always been so. In the twentieth century there were plenty of theologians who questioned traditional beliefs. However, their work rarely gets mentioned in today's pulpits. I have never felt a divide between what is said from pulpits and what is said in lecture theatres was healthy; any proclamation from the pulpit ought to take account of sensible scholarship. But experience has taught me that too often this does not happen.

In this book, you will find an overview of some of the scholarship that once was essential sermon fodder, but which now tends to be kicked into the long grass by preachers. Soothing their flock and stifling critical examination may please some, but it will drive others away.

I believe the Church is taking a wrong turning, unintentionally requiring its adherents to abandon their intellect in favour of unquestioned belief. It is, after all, the Church of England: it should surely include those who come to their faith through their minds as well as through their hearts.

There is plenty of room in Christianity for sincere belief strengthened with intellectual rigour. So far, at no point have I found that honest questioning of how I should interpret elements of my faith has pushed me to a position where I no longer felt myself to be a Christian. I have not found the process to be one of opening up a can of worms, but rather a cleansed and healthy relationship with what I can truly and honestly believe with all my heart and mind.

In Lewis Carroll's *Through the Looking Glass*, the White Queen tells Alice that in her youth she could believe 'six impossible things before breakfast', and counsels Alice to practise the same skill. The Church of England seems all too frequently to require the same of its congregations. I hope this book might show that there is an alternative.

1

WHO IS THE AUTHOR?

Any person will be influenced by their experience, so it might be helpful to outline briefly some of the key factors that have influenced me over the years.

I did not come from a church-going family. It was at the suggestion of a friend that, at about the age of 12, I joined an evangelical Bible Class for boys run by an organisation known as Crusaders. I went mainly because there was a planned outing by my friend's group to Southampton Docks that I thought might be entertaining. It was from such unremarkable decisions that a career would finally emerge. In the 1950s, Crusaders provided not only membership of a group that met every Sunday afternoon and normally one evening during the week, but the national organisation also provided a series of camping holidays in the summers and house parties in the winters. From about the age of 13 I went on such holidays with other young people from all over England once or twice a year. They were fun, and Crusaders must be credited with providing healthy, enjoyable and sometimes even quite adventurous holidays. Under their auspices, I cycled round much of Northern Ireland and then, the following year, Holland and Belgium.

A core part of the day on such ventures and in the house parties was some biblical teaching given, inevitably, from an evangelical point of view. For me, it opened up an engagement with the world of religion that I had scarcely known before. I am not sure I was ever a particularly easy member of any group, a certain questioning and even sceptical spirit was always part of my make-up, but it certainly did give me over time a reasonable knowledge of the Bible. It also gave me a sense that religion was an important dimension to life, and an awareness of the reality of the love and forgiveness of God that has never completely left me, even though my understanding of what the word God might mean has changed quite a lot over the years.

In the sixth form, I chose for my A level subjects mathematics, physics and chemistry, mainly because at the time schools were pushing boys to science unless they had a very strong desire to do something else. I was not naturally a scientist, and in some ways have regretted that choice, but I made a slight rebellion in also asking my school that I might do A level divinity, then still with a largely biblical syllabus. I was allowed to do so on the understanding that I would essentially have to teach myself. It was enough, because I found myself far more interested in that than in physics and chemistry. In a parallel personal development, while the Crusader organisation showed many of the marks of a church, it was essentially only a boys' group and members were encouraged to make links with local churches. During my teenage years, I had tried various churches, including a Baptist and a Methodist one, but finally, when my family moved house, I settled on a local Church of England parish, and through it was confirmed.

That led to what was probably the most important decision of my early life, taken at the age of 17, to pursue the possibility of ordination in the Church of England. At the time, I would have talked of a sense of personal calling, although my subsequent experience of being involved in the selection of candidates for ministry has made me far more cautious about such language.

But certainly I believed then that some of the most intriguing questions about life have a strongly religious dimension to them. Devoting my life to such questions would, I thought, be a worthwhile thing to do. I believe that still and have never regretted the decision to be ordained.

On leaving school, I spent two years living in the Mayflower Centre in the East End of London run then by David Sheppard, later Bishop of Liverpool. Canning Town was a tough part of London and, extraordinarily, I was allowed by the local education authority to teach as an unqualified teacher, first in a Church of England primary school and then as a religious education specialist in a boys secondary modern school. Clearly, the LEA was desperate! In the secondary school, according to some of the staff, all of one class I taught were on probation, but the staff may have been teasing me knowing that I was trying to teach the boys something about the Bible. It was certainly a challenge for someone who up until then had only experienced a rather narrow middle-class suburban life. I learned much from my encounters in Canning Town and that school.

But it was not just a sociological challenge I experienced. While I was at the Mayflower in 1963, at the age of 20, I picked up and read in one sitting over an evening and late into the night *Honest to God* by John Robinson, then Bishop of Woolwich.[1] Just before its publication the author had written an article in *The Observer* given the title by a sub-editor 'Our Image of God Must Go'. Robinson was essentially arguing that God was not to be encountered as someone 'up there' or even 'out there', but rather in the very depths of all being. The book became a publishing sensation, going into five print runs in the first five weeks and being one of the best-selling theological books ever.

1 John A. T. Robinson (1963) *Honest to God*. London: SCM Press.

It irritated the traditionalists but excited the radicals, and I found it wonderfully liberating. Here was someone, and a bishop to boot, asking all the questions I was asking about the Christian Faith and more. I remember saying to a friend at the time that it was as though I had lived all my life in a two dimensional theological world and had moved into a three dimensional one. But as the encounter with Robinson's thought was invigorating and exciting for me, the scorn heaped on the book by some of those I had previously looked up to as theological teachers was the more devastating of my respect for them. It marked a decisive break in my theological loyalties, and particularly in my approach to evangelicalism.

By then I had decided I definitely wanted to study theology at university and, encouraged by a friend at the Mayflower, applied to Trinity College Cambridge. I was interviewed by the Dean of Chapel, Harry Williams, who was subsequently to become my tutor, and in the course of the interview he simply said, 'Well, of course you can come next year. I do not think there is any point in your mugging up your maths and science for the entrance examination.' I naturally agreed, but was completely amazed. I cannot imagine entering the College is so easy now. Having Harry as tutor was an enormous privilege. He had recently published *The True Wilderness*, a collection of sermons and other addresses that reflected his emergence from a period of psychological turmoil and breakdown. I believe it is one of the greatest books of spiritual insight of the twentieth century. In the introduction he wrote:

> I found it became impossible to propound an official point of view like a political speaker taking a party line. Such a procedure appeared so false to myself that the words would not come.

> Unless what I proposed to say came from the depths of my own experience, I was struck dumb.[2]

I cannot personally claim the same searingly honest personal psychological insight, but as an approach to the Christian religion I have always thought it had much to commend it. The mid 1960s was a particularly stimulating time to study theology at Cambridge, with the debate between traditionalists and radicals alive and well within the Divinity Faculty. I was particularly fortunate in the supervisors Harry arranged for me. They included John Hick, later Professor of Theology at Birmingham, Alec Vidler, Dean of King's College, and Maurice Wiles, then Dean of Clare and later Regius Professor of Divinity at Oxford. They much enlarged my theological horizons. Much of what I describe in the themes of the following chapters was opened up for me in my initial years in Cambridge.

From Trinity I went to Westcott House, a theological college, also in Cambridge, in the broadly Liberal Catholic tradition of Anglicanism, but I was able to spend part of my second year on a World Council of Churches' Scholarship in the Orthodox Theological Seminary in Bucharest in Romania. I went just after the 1968 invasion of Czechoslovakia by the Soviet Union. There was speculation at the time that the Soviet Union might invade Romania, not because it was pursuing the internal freedoms that Alexander Dubček wanted in Czechoslovakia, but because Nicolae Ceaușescu, the President of Romania, who was pretty hard-line in his internal policies, wanted to pursue a far more independent foreign policy than the Soviet Union would like. The feared invasion did not happen, and the Foreign Office agreed to recommend to Lambeth Palace that I could go to the seminary. It gave me a fascinating seven months when I was

---

2 Harry Williams (1965) *The True Wilderness*. London: Constable, p.8.

able to learn much about the Orthodox Church, which was the main purpose of the scholarship, but I also observed a very tightly controlled police state in action. It was very sinister in what it did to relationships between individuals, where trust could often not be relied upon.

I returned to Westcott for a final term and went from there to ordination in St Paul's Cathedral and a curacy in St John's Wood in London. My training vicar was Noel Perry-Gore, a remarkably warm and friendly man who was to retire before I left the parish. The notice board outside the church said that the church welcomed all who believed and all who doubted, and it lived up to that reputation. It was a very good place in which to learn the basic elements of being a public representative of the Church in an open and welcoming environment.

Towards the end of my curacy, I was offered a post as Chaplain back at my old college of Trinity. By then Harry Williams had left to become a monk, and John Robinson, the author of *Honest to God*, that had so influenced me earlier, had become Dean. I was offered the job so far in advance that I had the opportunity to spend six months abroad between leaving the curacy and going back to Cambridge. I had always thought the problem of poverty in the Third World a critical one, so took an opportunity of travelling to India. I spent six weeks travelling round northern India and then, in the summer of 1973, worked in a mission station in the newly independent Bangladesh for three months. I saw at quite close quarters the appalling problems of one of the poorest and most over-populated countries in the world. I had never thought the problems of the unequal distribution of this world could be solved easily, but it was a great shock to hear one aid worker say that in one sense the best thing that could happen to Bangladesh was a disease that decimated the population. I did not, and still do not, agree with him, but it was a salutary experience to reflect upon in the following five years back in Cambridge, living, by contrast, on the high table of one of the most privileged institutions in England. The contrast could not have been greater.

The primary task of being chaplain was essentially to be available as a sympathetic presence to undergraduates and other students as well as being publicly known as an Anglican priest. I enjoyed the role and made friendships in Cambridge that endure to this day, including with the girl who is now my wife. I have a great respect for Trinity as a place where the then Senior Bursar once said to an undergraduate group I arranged to meet him that he was in the conversion business, to convert wealth into academic excellence. The College does that remarkably well, but I am not sure that I ever wholly resolved in my mind the contrast between such a privileged existence and what I had known in Bangladesh before.

In those five years, no doubt partly because of my involvement with undergraduates in need, but also because of the turmoil my own experiences had generated within me, I became interested in the whole matter of psychotherapy. What made people tick, and how could anyone integrate within themselves pressures that might in other circumstances simply tear them apart? I never found any simple resolutions to those issues, although engagement with a Jungian psychotherapist at least provided a context in which to reflect honestly upon them. Towards the end of my time as chaplain, the opportunity came to work in Church House Westminster in the department dealing with the selection of candidates for ordination. As this would inevitably entail examining the motivation of others interested in the same areas as myself, I jumped at the chance. I was there for seven years, for the last three of them as Senior Selection Secretary, responsible for the administration of the selection system. The experience fuelled the desire to write the twentieth-century history of the selection and training of ordination candidates in the Church of England, but that took a long time to come to fruition. I only finally completed the research in my last job, and the book was published early in 2013. Towards the end of my time in Church House I was also appointed joint secretary of a working party on Team and Group Ministries, which turned out to be a wonderful preparation for becoming Team Rector of Grantham in Lincolnshire, where I spent the next ten years.

Being a parish priest gives an extraordinary entry into the life of a community, with two things standing out in my memory. The regular taking of funerals, often as many as four or five a week, brought me into contact with a huge number of the general population. It is sometimes said of clergy they are considered as good as the last funeral they took; in which case I was certainly regularly open to judgement. But the matter became more acute for me personally when my father died suddenly and unexpectedly towards the end of my first year in Grantham. That certainly caused me to reflect again on what I believed about life after death, a reflection further deepened when my mother died towards the end of my time in the parish. This is a matter to which I shall return in the chapter on 'The Last Things'.

A second engagement with the life of the town came through schools. I was a governor of five schools, in one case as Chairman of Governors, which certainly made me well known to many in the town who otherwise had relatively little contact with the church. The Rector of a church has a role that goes way beyond simply being the chaplain to a congregation, and although it was at times demanding I much valued that engagement with the wider community. Being responsible for a large team ministry serving a population of over 30,000, with seven churches, five team vicars, a full-time curate and various non-stipendiary clergy and readers was also in many ways a fascinating if at times complex experience. Almost exactly half way through my time in Grantham I was also elected to the General Synod, and I was to spend nearly 15 years as a member of that rather strange body, of which more in Chapter 11 on 'Freedom of Thought in the Church of England'. But for the purposes of this book having a regular preaching ministry to a significantly sized congregation was also informative. I discovered what I had always suspected: that to raise some of the difficult questions about faith and even to suggest some responses that might be described as 'liberal' might upset a few people, but far more of the congregation were simply mightily relieved.

After a somewhat frustrating time wondering what I might do next – moving jobs in the Church of England is not a simple or straightforward experience – I was invited by the Bishop of Guildford to become Archdeacon of Surrey, and spent just over eight years engaging with the parishes and clergy in the western half of Guildford Diocese. Of course, there were some parishes where the clergy were far more conservative in their theological outlook than I was, although experience of some of the laity in their parishes made me wonder how far that conservatism was shared by their laity, while certainly among the clergy there were also many of a questioning and even radical temperament who responded very positively to some of the matters I raise later in this book. While in Surrey I was also given the opportunity to spend a three-month sabbatical to reflect further on the problem of believing in God in the face of the suffering of the world, and I did so in the context of looking at what the Holocaust did to Jewish ideas of God. It was a fascinating if, at times, harrowing investigation, and marks of it will be seen in what follows.

It did, though, finally confirm me in the notion, shared I found with a number of Jewish teachers, that you could believe in God without believing that He intervened in the world. It was only later that I discovered Maurice Wiles, my former supervisor, came to a similar conclusion in his Bampton Lectures for 1986 published as *God's Action in the World*.[3]

In Surrey, I was also very fortunate in many of my senior colleagues, and it was personally a happy time; but I was not sure I wanted to remain an Archdeacon for what could have been 17 years. I tentatively investigated a number of possibilities, but the final change was a surprise. In 2005, I was invited to move to Westminster Abbey as Canon Treasurer, which gave me oversight of the finances and care of the fabric of the Abbey. Being an Archdeacon was perhaps a good preparation for that role, made the easier by the fact that there were a number of highly competent and able lay people on the Abbey's staff whose experience and advice are second to none.

Westminster Abbey is an extraordinary place to work, not just because of the ability of colleagues lay and ordained, but also because of the remarkable range of people one encounters. Among them are those who are very distinguished and important; but every day in the Abbey there is a huge range of visitors from all over the world and from a wide variety of backgrounds, many of whom choose to come to services. To them the clergy can at least say goodbye, but in some cases have the chance of rather longer conversations. That is particularly the case after Sunday Matins, at which the Canon-in-Residence usually preaches. Each of the four Canons has to be 'in residence' for three months of the year, so he or she normally has to preach on about 13 occasions each year to the Matins congregation

3 Maurice Wiles (1986) *God's Action in the World: The Bampton Lectures for 1986.* London: SCM Press.

in addition to taking a turn with all their other colleagues in preaching, celebrating or assisting at the Eucharist throughout the rest of the year. Much of what follows in this book was tried out in various ways in my sermons in the Abbey over eight years. The reactions I have received simply further convinced me that honestly raising some of the difficulties about Christian Faith, and seeking to find responses consistent with contemporary knowledge in other areas of life, is for many people liberating rather than destructive.

It is with that conviction that I write this book. I am sure some will deeply disagree with some of my conclusions, including some respected former colleagues whom I still consider friends. But then disagreement within the Church is what makes it alive and interesting.

For further reading

Robinson, John A.T. (1963) *Honest to God.* London: SCM Press.

Wiles, Maurice (1986) *God's Action in the World: The Bampton Lectures for 1986.* London: SCM Press.

Williams, Harry (1965) *The True Wilderness.* London: Constable.

2

WHY SCEPTICISM?

Scepticism about religious belief has been present throughout human history, at least since Socrates. But particularly in the latter half of the nineteenth century and then throughout the twentieth it was occasioned by at least four factors.

Science

Science increasingly offered an explanation of how things happen that did not depend on supernatural acts of God. In a pre-scientific age, it was not surprising that remarkable natural phenomena were attributed to God. Storm and tempest, drought and flood, earthquake and eclipse were seen as examples of God's intervention in the natural world, and invocations to God to avoid such disasters were completely understandable. In our modern world, such theological explanations are far less easy to uphold. Once the explanation of an eclipse, for example, became clear, and accurate predictions of them became possible, these could no longer be described as some remarkable signs from God. As human knowledge advanced, and such explanations for how things happened developed, any recourse to God to intervene in the natural world became far less easy to imagine. The more science discovers how things happen, the less room there is for some sort of interventionist

God to provide an explanation for gaps in human knowledge, even though the range of what we do not know remains vast.

An illustration of that change became evident to me in a very practical way. When I was about to leave Westminster Abbey, my wife and I gave a party for many of our London-based friends, and, as part of the entertainment, we hired a magician who took groups of about eight to ten people into the library of our house and amazed them by the tricks he performed, sometimes with cards, sometimes predicting words in various pages of the books in the library. Everybody who went in was very impressed by his skill, and nobody could explain how he achieved the remarkable feats he did. But equally, nobody thought he did it by any form of supernatural magic. None of us could see the explanation, but we were all convinced that there was an explanation, and that his extraordinary skill was simply to make that explanation completely opaque. I could not help reflecting that, a few hundred years before, the reactions might have been different. Most people today do not believe in magic.

That highlights the vastly lessening sphere for the activity of any 'God of the gaps' in human knowledge, which is undoubtedly one reason for the weakened hold of some sorts of religious belief. It certainly lies behind the questioning of any statement that some specific act was miraculous, in the sense that divine intervention brought it about. It also accounts for many people's scepticism about events described as miracles in the Bible, because our contemporary experience of the world leads us to think that, if events are investigated carefully enough, a rational explanation can normally be discovered for how they happened.

In responding to such scientific advances, leading figures in the Church have often been far more sympathetic to scientific discoveries than popular imagination might think. Sir Charles

Lyell was Professor of Geology at King's College, London and remained a devout Anglican all his life. He died in 1875, but had no difficulty thinking that the universe was far older than conventional religion asserted, at least in the earlier part of that century and he was widely supported by many Christians at the time. Frederick Temple, Archbishop of Canterbury from 1896 to 1902, gave a series of lectures in 1884 on Science and Religion in which he stated that 'the doctrine of Evolution is in no sense whatever antagonistic to the teachings of Religion.'[1] Many leading churchmen at the time agreed with him, which was why it was not difficult for the then Dean of Westminster to allow Charles Darwin to be buried in the Abbey. A creative engagement between science and religion continued for most of the twentieth century, with many distinguished scientists being publicly known as Christians. Of course, there were always some in the scientific world who were non-believers, just as there were in the non-scientific world; but it was not automatically assumed that any good scientist would be an atheist.

For some scientists, that is now their assumption, and the attack on religion by the new atheists is one religious people cannot ignore. However, the new so-called conflict between science and religion is much more a conflict between some religious people and some scientists, both of whom often claim far too much for their discipline and sometimes, sadly, caricature their opponents. Some Christians have certainly made extraordinary claims for the authority of some bit of religious teaching from their scriptures, although such claims are far from universal among believers, many of whom are quite happy to accept the scientific explanation for how something

1 Frederick Temple (1884) *The Relations between Religion and Science: Eight Lectures Preached Before the University of Oxford in the Year 1884*. London: Macmillan, p.107.

came about. As regards questioning the stance of some scientists, Cardinal Cormac Murphy O'Connor, when he was the Roman Catholic Archbishop of Westminster, asked his audience in a lecture in his cathedral whether any of them knew anyone who believed in the God that Richard Dawkins did not believe in. He commented, 'The God that is being rejected by such people is a God I don't believe in either. I simply don't recognise my faith in what is presented by these critics as Christian faith.'[2] Neither do I.

It is interesting to observe that those scientists that refuse to have anyone who describes themselves as a Christian in their research departments, on the grounds that they could not be good scientists if they held that belief, are simply mirroring the stance of the Inquisition. It was then held that those who were not Christians had such a fundamental lack of judgement that they should not be allowed to continue their work. Exponents of both science and religion can display a deeply unattractive dogmatism.

Jonathan Sacks, the former Chief Rabbi, considered a more creative way in which science and religion might engage in his book *The Great Partnership*. He suggested that while it is the job of science to take things apart to see how they work, it is the job of religion to put things together to see what they mean. In the first area, science is obviously king, but in taking things apart to see how they work there is an assumption that the physical world operates in a reasonably ordered and coherent way susceptible to careful observation and analysis. Most Christians today have no difficulty in believing that, although the subsequent question about miracles still applies.

---

2 This quotation appeared on the Westminster Cathedral website shortly after the lecture was given. It is no longer there.

But what about Sacks's second proposition that it is the job of religion to put things together to see what they mean? An Anglican theologian of the mid twentieth century, Austin Farrer (1904-68), suggested there could be something he described as 'double agency',[3] when the natural cause for something could be seen as being part of a wider divine action. It is a notion worth reflecting upon.

The apparently natural process of healing in the human body could be seen as an example. It does not require any sort of divine intervention to bring it about: the tendency to heal just happens to be one of the natural processes in the world. God is not wheeled in as some sort of separate force, sometimes operating and sometimes not operating within the healing process. For the believer, God is simply the ultimate cause of all that is, which includes the natural ability of the body to heal itself. The process of healing is therefore part of an entirely proper scientific inquiry. But the fact that this is a world where healing is both possible and natural, and that there is such a process for doctors to cooperate with in order to facilitate health, may point to something about life itself that shows it might be made in such a way to fulfil the purposes of God.

'Double agency' is also possible when we examine actions of human beings. People's belief in God can be the motivating force that makes them behave as they do in a specific situation. Some saw the collapse of apartheid in South Africa as remarkable and even miraculous, but it was brought about by human beings behaving in response to what they saw as God's demand for justice and honesty. In that sense, it is possible to speak sensibly

3 Austin Farrer used the phrase in the Preface to *Faith and Speculation* (London: A and C Black, 1967, p. v) where he spoke of 'double agency, divine and creaturely'. A fuller exploration of the idea is contained in *Saving Belief*, mentioned in the Further Reading although he does not use the phrase 'double agency' there.

about God working in and through some people, without requiring any notion of divine intervention.

Does that have consequences for how we can perceive the miraculous? Something that evokes wonder, amazement and gratitude may be described as miraculous, precisely because it produces those reactions in the observers. That does not mean that there must be something magical about what brought it about. Miraculous does not mean magical. A wholly rational investigation of how something came about is not inconsistent with it evoking a sense of wonder. So 'double agency' can have some sort of meaning and miraculous need not refer to how something happened, but rather to what it evokes in the observer. Sacks's notion that religion is about putting things together to see what they mean makes sense, because it provokes the fundamental question, 'Just what sort of universe do we live in?'

Scientific method has had the effect of changing how many Christians conceive of God. Unlike the biblical picture of God as a force acting through details of the natural world, God can be seen rather as the reason why anything is here in the first place. Such a view has dimensions that point to the nature of what God is like, and responding to God can indeed be a positive force in the world. I say more about that in the next chapter.

There is one further dimension to any scientific understanding that might affect Christian belief, and that is in the fundamental question of 'what is a human being?' For a long time it was quite possible to assume that human beings consisted of a body, mind and spirit, and such a perception underlay a good deal of Christian thought in an earlier period. However, now many would hold that our understanding of being human has changed, and humans are seen as a psychosomatic unity, with mind and body intimately bound together. That raises the question of whether what used to be called the spirit or even the soul has any independent existence apart from the physical mind. This too I discuss in the next chapter and then later in Chapter 8. Personally I do not think that undermines Christian belief, but it does mean it needs to be recast in a somewhat different mould. That is yet another way in which scientific explanations of aspects of life inevitably challenge and sometimes change the way any Christian might think about their faith.

Biblical Criticism

A second development that happened from about the eighteenth century involved approaches to the Bible. The traditional description of the Bible as the Word of God was taken to mean by some Christians that all its contents were literally and absolutely correct. That was certainly not a universal view. In much earlier periods of the Christian Church, a far wider range of ways of interpreting the Bible was often used. The fundamentalism that treats the Bible as inerrant in describing historical events is a relatively recent development, dating from the early twentieth century.

But by then, another challenge had come to the fore – Biblical Criticism. Could the Bible be studied using the same critical methods that scholarship used to study other ancient texts? That involved considering such matters as who the authors were, in what circumstances their documents were produced, what might have influenced their writing and what their primary purposes in writing were. Many thinking Christians certainly believed such methods should indeed be applied to both the Old and New Testaments, and that led to questioning whether the history told in both was necessarily as accurate as had previously been assumed.

For the Old Testament, Biblical Criticism mainly began with an examination of the Pentateuch, or first five books of the Old Testament, and the Book of Joshua. Tradition had assigned the authorship of the Pentateuch to Moses, but that was clearly problematical when one of the books describes Moses' own death. Certain differences in style in different parts of each book, the use made of different names for God (Yahweh and Elohim) and the very different character of some of the sections led to the emergence of what became known as the Graf–Wellhausen hypothesis, named after two German scholars, Karl Heinrich Graf (1815–69) and Julius Wellhausen (1844–1918). Writing in the 1870s, Wellhausen saw the books as an amalgamation of a number of different writings, each reflecting different traditions within Judaism over a number of centuries. That view lasted the best part of a century and has only been modified by the suggestions that there may be more or less than the original four strands that Wellhausen proposed. But the essential point is that such a way of looking at those Old Testament books made it clear that they were a human creation, albeit one possibly revealing something of the nature of God. That allowed a way of looking at the first few chapters of Genesis that saw them, not as an historical account of the creation of the world, but as a far more theological interpretation told through the use of myth.

Such a way of looking at the first books of the Old Testament is probably uncontroversial for many in the Church today, but what is perhaps less common amongst those in the pews is an equally questioning approach to some of the Old Testament books of prophecy. Years of listening to Gospel stories about Jesus' birth interpreted in terms of Old Testament prophecy have had their effect, yet any careful examination of those texts shows that the interaction between the Old and New Testaments is far more complex. Reading the Old Testament texts in their original context often shows that their meaning was relating to something contemporary to their writing, rather than something far into the future. Also, there remains the question of whether the Gospel authors, having decided that some particular Old Testament passage applied to Jesus, then told their own story to reflect that belief, rather than because they believed it to be historically true. Examples of this will be discussed in greater detail in Chapter 4 on Jesus.

Methods of Biblical Criticism were also applied to the New Testament. An eighteenth-century German Enlightenment philosopher, Hermann Reimarus (1694–1768), studied the Gospels carefully using the same methods he would have applied to any other ancient text, and came to the conclusion that the Gospels could not be accepted uncritically as historically accurate. That provoked a long scholarly discussion, initially mainly in Germany but then on a much wider scale, about how the New Testament came to be written and what the balance was between history, legend and interpretation. That debate continues today.

What is not contentious now is the recognition that the first books of the New Testament were not the Gospels but the letters of the apostle Paul, written at various stages from about 51 AD to Paul's death, probably about 65 AD. There are 13 letters in the New Testament attributed to Paul, but there is scholarly debate about their authenticity. The majority of scholars conclude that seven of them were genuinely by Paul, but of the rest the authorship is much contested, with the possibility that some were later documents attributed to Paul, as was common practice in the ancient world.

The dating of the Gospels is also much discussed. The vast majority of New Testament scholars agree that the first Gospel to be written was Mark, followed by Matthew and Luke, and finally John – although some seek to give an earlier date to John's Gospel. What is generally accepted is that Matthew and Luke both had Mark's material before them as they wrote, and there is additional material in both Matthew and Luke so close in structure and language that there may well have been a common source, written or otherwise. John's Gospel does appear to be a more independent composition, with widely varying opinions on when it was written and by whom.

The one date that is certain in the whole period is that in 70 AD the Romans sacked Jerusalem, destroyed the Temple and carried out a savage butchery of the Jewish population. There is debate as to whether or not that is reflected in any of the Gospels. Many believe it was, in Matthew 24 and Luke 19. These therefore date Matthew and Luke after that event, but with Mark's Gospel possibly completed before that in the later 60s. Some, however, including Bishop John Robinson, argue an earlier date for all the Gospels. There is no universal scholarly consensus.

This whole critical approach to the Bible has generated a vast range of scholarly material, which it would be foolish to attempt to summarise here. But it does all lead to a measure of uncertainty about how to evaluate the biblical evidence. Particular accounts of events or the sayings of Jesus develop as different Gospel writers tell them. Why were those changes made? Was it that new evidence came to light, which made the author feel earlier attempts were somehow wrong or at least incomplete historically, or was it, as seems more likely, that in the light of what was happening in the Church the author knew about he saw that words or actions of Jesus could be given a different and maybe new significance? A classic example would be the statement of Jesus in Luke's Gospel, 'Blessed are you poor, for yours is the Kingdom of God', which in Matthew is, 'Blessed are the poor in spirit, for theirs is the kingdom of heaven.' Did Matthew add 'in spirit' because the church he knew was one with wealthy members, and he wanted to make Jesus' words applicable even to the wealthy, or did Luke remove the words because he wanted to emphasise Jesus' commitment to the financially poor? We simply do not know. Such uncertainty about the original meaning is present in many of the Gospel sayings and actions of Jesus, which makes searching for the meaning fascinating, but also raises big questions about interpreting the New Testament.

Historical Scepticism

The third factor that affected approaches to the biblical tradition stems partly from an amalgamation of the first two. Both scientific developments and Biblical Studies led to a measure of scepticism about the historical accuracy of many biblical stories. The general truths science has discovered in seeing how things happen through 'taking them apart' presumably applied even before those truths were understood, and asserting the truth of statements that seem now historically and scientifically highly unlikely is, to say the least, problematic. Of course, some Christians appear to have no difficulty in accepting the literal accuracy of all biblical stories, but there are many others who bring a high degree of scepticism to the process. The answer to the question 'What really happened?' is never going to be easy. Some things are inevitably lost in the mists of history and only a foolish person would claim certainty about almost any text, but the question retains its fascination and force.

This issue comes to the fore in those books in the New Testament that appear historical – the Gospels and the Acts of the Apostles. Some scholars argue for their substantial historical authenticity, but others believe the accounts themselves have been so influenced by the situation in the local church where they were finally written down that it is now almost impossible to distinguish between what is history and what is later interpretation. It is certainly possible to look at passages from Mark to see how Matthew and Luke treated them, and to recognise that both Matthew and Luke could be fairly free with their sources. What is much more difficult to get behind is where the material in Mark's Gospel came from in the first place. If, as many scholars hold, Mark's book was not written until the mid to late 60s, then there was a thirty-odd-year period between the death of Jesus and the Gospel being written. What happened in that period of oral tradition, and how the stories were modified and retold, is certainly open to question, particularly as modern methods of assessing historical accounts were not available then. Any Gospel writer's telling of history required selection to identify what they thought really was significant and lasting. For the authors of the New Testament, what was important was preaching the Gospel and conveying the message and meaning of Jesus Christ. They were not twenty-first-century historians, and critical analysis of what actually happened was not central to their purpose. It is also evident that the events recorded in the Gospels only account for a very small part of Jesus' life. If, as many believe, he was about 33 when he died, what is told in the Gospels would only take up a few weeks. The simple fact remains that we have only an incomplete and not entirely reliable account of his life.

There is no scholarly unanimity on any of these issues. At the more radical end of the spectrum of Christian belief is

The Jesus Seminar, a group of New Testament scholars based in the United States, who question whether many of the sayings attributed to Jesus in the Gospels were actually spoken by the historical Jesus. More conservative scholars question their scepticism. But what is clear is that questioning the historical accuracy of some of the material in the Gospels is not simply the preserve of radical and liberal scholars; there is genuine wide and real disagreement.

This obviously creates a difficulty for those who hold that acceptance of the facts related in the Gospels is necessary for Christian belief. That applies especially to the stories of the resurrection of Jesus, where the contrasts between the different Gospel accounts of the resurrection are striking. I discuss them at greater length in Chapter 5. But since this is the central 'historical fact' on which much Christian belief is based, then if there are good literary and historical reasons for questioning what lay behind these very different accounts, it does raise problems for those who feel compelled to maintain some sort of intellectual integrity in the face of this uncertainty. There are some Christian scholars who find ways to absorb all those differences in the Gospels and assert that there can be no doubt about what actually happened, but, as I illustrate later, there are other equally serious Christian scholars who question aspects of that. In any case, the fact that those scholars who assert the literal truth of the resurrection approach it as Christians does make an objective observer wonder whether their prior belief influences their conclusions, rather than the other way round. I say more about that in the section on Psychological Scepticism that follows.

As one who is by temperament in the sceptical camp, I can only believe far more honesty from the pulpit about the difficulties of historical certainty regarding the Bible in general, and the Gospel stories in particular, could only be for the good of the Church's intellectual credibility. Sadly, I have rarely heard this honesty. The gap between lecture room and pulpit seems as great as ever.

Psychological Scepticism

A fourth factor that underlies the questioning of Christian approaches to truth is the recognition of the role of the unconscious, largely flowing from the work of Freud, Jung and other twentieth-century psychologists. Human beings are not desiccated thinking machines. We may well find what we think are good and sound reasons for holding a particular point of view on something, but our psychological make-up, our fears and hopes, our feelings and our sufferings inevitably influence our thinking processes as well as our conclusions. This applies to all human beings. I am certainly not saying that Christians are more dishonest about this than anyone else, but why anybody believes any particular thing is a complex matter. It requires some investigation, at least by the individuals themselves, into what those psychological pressures might be. The problem is that by their very nature many psychological processes happen in the unconscious, so understanding how these processes affect us is always difficult.

Perhaps it is easier to speculate about others than to know that much about oneself. Some display characteristics that reveal to the observer that behind their very definite and certain stance on an issue there are inner uncertainties, which are not known or at least not publically acknowledged by the individual concerned. Is the rigid stance of someone on some issue determined by a rigorous intellectual process, or by unconscious forces moulding and making them the people they are? Once it is recognised that such processes are at work in everyone then each individual can begin to question him or herself, and certainly to question others' certainties.

I must, of course, apply that to myself. Did my original commitment to being a Christian owe much to personal psychological factors? Yes, definitely. My teenage experience was not simply an intellectual decision; there were undoubtedly deep emotional elements in it as well. Are there emotional elements involved in my more current sceptical position? Yes, although my movement towards a greater scepticism has been a long process lasting a number of years, which I hope has involved careful thought as well as feelings. Does that mean my holding on to Christianity now is actually a clinging on to a belief system that provided a security that I am now reluctant to abandon? Well, maybe, although I stand by what I said in the preface that I certainly still count myself as a Christian. I hope in the chapters that follow to explain what I do now believe and why I think it is still a coherent basis for living as a Christian, taking part in Christian worship with conviction and, I hope, behaving as a Christian. But psychological scepticism about why people say they believe what they believe is part of a general contemporary scepticism. The Church cannot be immune from those pressures.

Conclusion

For all these reasons, and possibly for others as well, the Christian Church has to face the fact that many in our society are questioning or doubtful about many Christian beliefs. I believe those questions and doubts can be honestly faced, with the factors that lie behind them engaged with sympathetically. That is the purpose of this book.

For further reading

Science

Ian Barbour (2002) *Nature, Human Nature and God.* London: SPCK.

Austin Farrer (1964) *Saving Belief.* London: Hodder and Stoughton.

John Hick (2010) *The New Frontier of Religion and Science.* Basingstoke: Palgrave Macmillan.

Arthur Peacock (2000) 'Science and the Future of Theology: Critical Issues' *Zygon 35* (2000), pp.119–40.

John Polkinghorne (1996) *Scientists as Theologians.* London: SPCK.

Jonathan Sacks (2011) *The Great Partnership: God, Science and the Search for Meaning.* London: Hodder and Stoughton.

Biblical Criticism and Historical Scepticism

J.L. Houlden (1992) *Jesus: A Question of Identity.* London: SPCK.

Keith Ward, (2004) *What the Bible Really Teaches: A Challenge for Fundamentalists.* London: SPCK.

Maurice Wiles (1999) *Reason to Believe.* London: SCM.

Psychological Scepticism

Sigmund Freud (2008, first published in 1928) *The Future of an Illusion.* London: Penguin.

William James (1977, first published in 1902) *The Varieties of Religious Experience.* London: Fount Paperback.

C.G. Jung (1961, first published in 1933) *Modern Man in Search of a Soul.* London: Routledge and Keegan Paul.

3

WHAT DOES IT MEAN TO BELIEVE IN GOD?

Some years ago one of the translators of the New Testament into modern English, J.B. Phillips, wrote a book called *Your God is Too Small.*[1] It was a good title, because some often have far too limited a notion of God. They appear to start with a mental image of what we might mean by God that almost makes him into an object within the universe, which may or may not exist. Indeed, such a limited vision of God apparently lies behind the thought of many of the new advocates of atheism. Their vision of what Christians believe about God is an Aunt Sally they define in such a way that their notion of God can easily be knocked down, but it is far removed from what many thoughtful Christians believe. Some of the medieval theologians used to say that God was beyond being. They were suggesting that we should never talk in such simplistic terms as whether God existed or not, for he is the condition for anything existing.

Lord Rees, the former President of the Royal Society and Astronomer Royal, started his book *Our Cosmic Habitat* by saying, 'The pre-eminent mystery is why anything exists at all.'[2] It is a mystery worth pondering upon. Why is there a universe, the

1 J.B. Phillips (1965) *Your God is Too Small.* London: Wyvern Books.

2 Martin Rees (2002) *Our Cosmic Habitat.* London: Weidenfeld and Nicholson, p.1.

real mysteries of which we are only beginning to understand? It is possible to start with a definition of God that says simply that God is the word we use as the condition of why anything is at all. It is a very imperfect description, but it does show why those medieval theologians could speak so powerfully of the 'mystery' of God. Those who try to speak about God should never forget that the very concept is so much beyond our understanding that any knowledge we might claim of him can only be at best provisional. A measure of humility before the notion of God is surely an essential starting point.

But the developments that have occurred in cosmologists' understanding of how the universe and the world came to be, and of those who have shown how evolution explains much of the emergence of life and human beings in particular, does undermine many of the traditional arguments for the existence of God as the initial creator. Wheeling in the notion of God as some sort of explanation of how the universe came to be has become less necessary. Many cosmologists now, including Martin Rees, think it is quite possible that there are multiple universes. He wrote:

> The multiverse concept is already part of empirical science: we may already have intimations of other universes… In an infinite ensemble, the existences of some universes that are seemingly fine-tuned to harbour life would occasion no surprise: our own cosmic habitat would plainly belong to this unusual subset. Our entire universe is a fertile oasis within the multiverse.[3]

It may not have been one big bang, but many, far distant from our universe. One theologian, John Hick a former Professor of Theology at Birmingham, acknowledged the issue:

---

3 Rees, *Our Cosmic Habitat*, p.xvii.

> The science/religion debate used to turn on whether the universe's 'fine-tuned' state was so improbable as to require purposeful divine action to have brought about the stars, planets and life as we know it. This is countered by the multiverse theory, which reduces the improbability to near zero by seeing our universe as one of perhaps billions of universes, among which it is not at all improbable that there should be one, or indeed a number, that happened to produce intelligent life.[4]

With such a view it is arguable that the conditions that make life possible on earth are just a consequence of happenstance. The conditions for the universe(s) existing at all and the conditions for human life evolving on earth are extraordinary, but some sort of divine hand is not a necessary explanation. That need not stop those who say they believe in God seeing him as the ultimate creator and sustainer of all that is, but they do need to accept that it is not an automatic belief for anyone who looks at the science in the present state of scientific knowledge.

But if we start with the notion of God, not as an explanation of how the universe came to be, but as the word we use for why it exists at all, we can see that developing any sort of relationship with him is actually about developing a relationship with the universe of which we are a part. What do we feel about this cosmic habitat in which we are set? Just to ask the question is to be plunged into mystery, but we can also see that it is fundamental. How do we relate to everything, and to whatever it is that is at the heart of everything? What do we feel about existing at all? If that is what religion is about, then although some religious responses have clearly been inadequate in the face of the hugeness of the issue, it does shift the question from 'how?' to 'why?'

---

4 John Hick (2010) *The New Frontier of Religion and Science*. Basingstoke: Palgrave Macmillan, p.xi.

With that in mind, and with the basic intellectual humility we need in considering the question of God at all carefully, what more dare we say about him? Are there elements in life that point more naturally to what the idea of God might be about? Jonathan Sacks said it was the job of science to take things apart to see how they work, but it was the job of religion to put things together to see what they mean. If Sacks is right about the role of science, then we must allow that scientists who do not see a need for God to explain the existence of the universe have a point. But if Sacks is also right about religion putting things together to see what they mean, then what needs to be put together to point to some notion of a God that is believable and gives meaning? There are at least four things that appear to be fundamental to human living and which might be related in some way to the notion of God.

The first is the extraordinary phenomenon of consciousness. Not only do human beings exist, but we are capable of thinking carefully about our existence and reflecting upon its meaning. The relationship between the brain and the mind is a hugely complex issue that is only beginning to be understood, but the extraordinary thing about our minds and our consciousness is that while they are unique to each individual – none of us can fully understand the consciousness of another – nonetheless we communicate, and in that process influence the minds of others and are in turn influenced by them. In the process of thinking about the world we find a way of trying to make sense of it, to understand it and even to formulate some laws on how it works. Even more than that, we are then capable of reflecting on how we behave, deciding what sort of contribution we might make through our lives to the whole human enterprise, and how to make it. Each person has some role, however minimal, in making the world of the future.

The American philosopher David Bentley Hart makes much of this in his book *The Experience of God,* where he suggests that consciousness as we conceive of it is irreconcilable with a materialistic view of reality. He believes that a convinced materialist will see everything, even the most abstract concepts that might exist in the mind and in consciousness, as entirely mechanical in the brain's neurological processes, yet he believes that to be a 'fundamental and incorrigible conceptual confusion'.[5] He states that it is a principle of the mechanistic vision of reality that material forces are essentially mindless, intrinsically devoid of purpose, and that complex rational organisation is not a property naturally residing in material reality. It can only be imposed upon material reality. 'Consciousness would appear to be everything that, according to the principles of mechanism, matter is not: directed, purposive, essentially rational.'[6] And for this reason he concludes: 'The difference in kind between the material structure of the brain and the subjective structure of consciousness remains fixed and inviolable, and so the precise relation between them cannot be defined, or even isolated as an object of scientific scrutiny.'[7] It is a complex argument well worth engaging with, and when he goes on to reject what some neuroscientists suggest, that we are sheer automatons with no free well, he is surely right. The experience of having a measure of free will is so deep in human consciousness that to dismiss it as an artificial creation of our mechanical brains must be wrong.

John Hick also thinks that religion's fundamental debate is with materialism, or what he calls physicalism. He agrees with neuroscientists when they say that 'everything going

---

5 David Bentley Hart (2013) *The Experience of God* London: Yale University Press, p.154.

6 Hart, *Experience of God*, p.154.

7 Hart, *Experience of God*, p.157.

on in consciousness is also going on in the brain. There is complete consciousness-brain correlation.' But he suggests that 'correlation does not mean identity'. The brain is not the same thing as the mind or consciousness. And he notes that some leading neuroscientists admit that the nature of consciousness is a sheer mystery.[8]

Bentley Hart notes that in an earlier stage of human thinking this led to a demarcation between the distinct realms of material mechanism and rational soul, but that more recently many have adopted a conception that the material world is the only real world and everything must be explained in its terms. This is very clearly stated in a book entitled *Do No Harm* by the brain surgeon Henry Marsh. The subtitle is *Stories of Life, Death and Brain Surgery*, which gives an extraordinary insight into a brain surgeon's work. At one point he makes the following observation.

> Neuroscience tells us that it is highly improbable that we have souls, as everything we think and feel is no more or no less than the electrochemical chatter of our nerve cells. Our sense of self, our feelings and our thoughts, our love for others, our hopes and ambitions, our hates and fears all die when our brains die. Many people deeply resent this view of things, which not only deprives us of life after death but also seems to downgrade thoughts to mere electrochemistry and reduces us to no more than automats or machines. Such people are profoundly mistaken, since what it really does is upgrade matter into something infinitely mysterious that we do not understand. There are a hundred billion nerve cells in our brains. Does each one have a fragment of consciousness within it? How many nerve cells do we require to be conscious or to feel pain? Or does consciousness and thought reside in the electrochemical impulses that join those

8 Hick, *New Frontier*, p.xiv.

billion of cells together? Is a snail aware? Does it feel pain when you crush it underfoot? Nobody knows.[9]

I am sure Bentley Hart is right about the change in intellectual fashion – many now conceive of a human being as a psychosomatic unity – but personally I share that now fashionable view. To that extent I believe Marsh is probably right. I do not understand at all how my brain manages to create my mind with its views of how the world is and how I relate to others, but I am far from certain that my mind and my consciousness exist independent of my brain. At the end of the day, our brains are material objects through which our minds and our consciousness are perceived. I shall discuss what Marsh says about life after death in a later chapter, but whether you are a materialist or not, the existence of minds and our consciousness remains a mysterious and fascinating fact. It is the first factor I wish to put into that melting pot that might make sense of the notion of God, and how our consciousness relates to any notion of God.

The second factor is the pursuit of truth. What is truth and what claim does it make on us? I fear religious believers must admit that at times religions have laid claim to knowing and guarding truth, but have often done so in blinkered, untruthful and harmful ways. But it is not only religions that have done that; all sorts of other groups who wanted to harness the power of ideas have tried to control the process: look at Fascist and some Communist systems. The open pursuit of truth is dangerous to almost all ideologies, especially those that assume infallibility.

Even without any ideological commitment, it is also very easy to collude in evasion. T.S. Eliot once wrote, 'Human kind

9 Henry Marsh (2014) *Do No Harm: Stories of Life, Death and Brain Surgery*. London: Weidenfeld and Nicholson, p.200.

cannot bear very much reality.'[10] Many would prefer to settle for the comfortable rather than for the truthful. Yet for some other people there remains a desperate urge to pursue truth whatever the cost. Where does the pressure to pursue truth in such a single-minded way come from? Is it just the human creation of curious and honest men and women? Or is it somehow written into the very nature of the universe? Some people seem to experience the need to pursue truth as a response to some sort of transcendent, overarching claim. For me, that claim is rooted in the condition of everything that I call God. God and truth are not separate; if you have a big enough concept of God they are intimately connected, and the search for one is the search for the other. This is certainly not to say that only those who believe in God pursue truth; manifestly that is not the case, for there are many serious searchers after truth that describe themselves as atheists. But it is the transcendent, overarching nature of the pressure to pursue truth that fascinates me. It certainly does not prove the existence of God to the honest doubter, but it may show something of what believing in God might mean. If pursuing truth is seeking to understand the nature of the universe of which we are a part, and if you understand the word God simply to mean whatever is the ultimate reality that is at the heart of everything, then pursuing one is pursuing the other.

The third of the factors and in many ways a similar issue is the claim of goodness. Of course what is considered good has varied at different times of human history, and, as with truth, various groups, including religious bodies, have tried to control society's understanding of it. Yet most thinking people will know that what is good in any particular situation is a complex and difficult question, not least because it often entails making

---

10 'Burnt Norton' in 'Four Quartets', in T. S. Eliot (1952) *The Complete Poems and Plays of T S Eliot.* London: Faber and Faber, p.172.

a choice between different goods. And it would seem that, for some people, the claim of goodness appears to exercise very little control over what they are; survival and personal enjoyment, for some, seem to be far more powerful motivators. Yet it remains that for many people there is also a strong drive to pursue good, not in some childish 'goodie, goodie' sense, but in a far more fundamental commitment to altruism in what they do with their lives. But where does the sense of obligation towards doing genuine and deep good come from? Again, it seems to have a transcendent claim upon us; the pursuit of goodness in its purest form, I suggest, is not merely a human construction. It, like truth, seems to be rooted in the very heart of the universe, or in what I am choosing to call God.

The fourth factor is possibly beauty, although that is more complex, because beauty even more than truth and goodness is at least to some extent culturally conditioned. It is sometimes said that beauty is simply in the eye of the beholder. But is that enough of an explanation? Can we really say that a piece of music, or an image from nature, or an image from the hands of human beings, or even a mathematical explanation, is merely beautiful because they seem so to us? The appeal of the sublime is deeply felt by many, and beauty, like truth and goodness, may, I believe, also be rooted in something greater than us. Again, for want of a better word, I am content to call that something God despite the problems of cultural relativity.

So the word God does seem to me to point to something, or someone, real – indeed so real that he is at the heart of everything. He is at that point in our consciousness where truth, goodness and beauty meet. It is not a question of believing in *a* personal God, but it is believing that in our understanding of everything there is God, and contained within the mystery of God is something that we can experience as personality.

In responding to the universe of which we are a part we can respond to it in personal terms. God is not the immediate cause of events that happen in the world like a sort of master puppeteer, but in responding to him people act in ways they might not otherwise have acted, and through them God may indeed be working his purposes out.

Within the Christian tradition there is also one other statement about God that is worth considering, namely that God is love. At the heart of everything, and the reason why anything exists in the first place, there is love, not as some sort of sentimental emotion, but a force that wants to enable human beings to live together in a creative and loving way and to see the world as a context in which such love can develop. There is, however, an immediate problem about relating to the universe and to any notion of God like that at the heart of it, and that is the fact of suffering.

Suffering comes about in some cases by natural disaster or disease. Earthquakes, tsunamis, cancer or cot deaths can all bring about a great questioning of God. But probably at least as much human suffering in the world is caused by the sheer wickedness of the way in which human beings can treat one another. When I spent some time looking at Jewish attitudes to God in the light of the Holocaust, I was much taken by the statement of an American Rabbi, Irving Greenberg, who had read the transcript of one of the Nuremberg trials relating to Auschwitz. Evidently at one stage the decision was taken by the Nazi authorities not to put young Jewish children into the gas chambers, but to throw them alive into the crematoria, and their screams were heard throughout the camp. Greenberg commented, 'No statement, theological or otherwise, should be made that could not be made with credibility in the presence of the burning children.'[11] I have sometimes thought that statement should be printed on the pulpit desk of every church as a caution to the preacher. Much suffering is truly terrible, and in the face of such suffering any believer in God must pause.

But at least, in the case of the Holocaust, there were other human beings who could, and should, be held responsible. Human beings have free will, and some have abused that free will dreadfully. The abuse of free will lies not only in the evil that is done, but in what is not done. Edmund Burke once said, 'The only thing necessary for the triumph of evil is for good men to do nothing.' Maybe we all bear some measure of culpability for the evil that is done in the world.

But there are other disasters that are not the responsibility of human beings, and where freewill cannot be used as an explanation, still less an excuse. The tsunami of Boxing Day 2004 resulted in over a quarter of a million people killed and well over a million people displaced. The Haiti earthquake of 2010 had very similar numbers of deaths and displacement. They were horrific natural disasters, and of course they raise the question of 'Where was God?'

That question was also asked in 1755 after the tragedy of the Lisbon earthquake, which killed up to 100,000 people. A very tough answer in the context of Lisbon was given in the last century by the Oxford theologian Austin Farrer, who said that God was there 'allowing the earth's crust to behave according to its nature.'[12] Much the same answer on the movement of tectonic plates could be given about the tsunami, and although very tough I suppose that answer is essentially true. The universe

---

11 Irving Greenberg (2001) 'Cloud of Smoke, Pillar of Fire', in Michael Morgan (ed.) (2001) *A Holocaust Reader*. Oxford: Oxford University Press, p.107f.

12 Austin Farrer (1966) *The Science of God*. London: Geoffrey Bles, p.87.

is as it is, and I am not sure that we can wish God had made it otherwise. Perhaps we need a world with the fact of human free will and the possibilities of challenge and tragedy if strong character is ever to be formed. If everything was just easy and there was no possibility of tragedy, maybe that would produce only easy and complacent character. Keats once described this world as 'a vale of soul-making'.

Personally, I think reflections like that show that it is very difficult to sustain any notion of God being a sort of master puppeteer, pulling the strings of the world to make things happen. God may be the reason why there is anything at all in the first place, but that does not mean he is reason for every single thing that happens thereafter. Of course, some Christians believe he is and suggest that natural disasters are a punishment on people for some wickedness. What any of the young children who died in a tsunami or Auschwitz can have done to deserve that is, I confess, completely beyond me. I find such expressions very difficult. If God is a master puppeteer like that, it seems to me he is nothing other than a monster, and certainly does not deserve our love or our respect.

But maybe God is not like that. Perhaps God is not all-powerful in the way some would suggest, because any act of creation carries with it an element of risk, as any parent will know. Love is not all-powerful, and it can be thwarted. Once something is created, whether it is a universe or a human being, it then has a life of its own and cannot be simply manipulated. In the case of our world, both because of the nature of the physical world and the nature of human beings, there is always the possibility of terrible tragedy and even disaster, and the question about God is, 'What will those who believe in Him do in response to such events?' The answer seems to be, thank God, that in many cases they strive to overcome the consequences and to re-build, learning the lessons of whatever disaster it was. To see where God was in an event like a natural disaster involves looking at two things: the practical love and compassion of those individuals and agencies who bring help and relief to those who are traumatised by the disaster; and the resilience, courage and determination shown by some of the victims who strive to live authentically even in the midst of tragedy in seeking to put their lives and the lives of their communities back together again. God may have been there in creating the world as it is, but he is also there in the victims, who are also part of his creation, creating the world as it will be.

No religious group has more claim to be listened to on this subject than the Jewish people after their experience of the Holocaust. One of the best-known witnesses of that was Elie Wiesel. He was brought up in the Transylvanian town of Sighet, the son of devout Jewish parents. As a boy he was fascinated by his religion, studying the Talmud and Kabbalah with extraordinary intensity. But at the age of 15 he, together with the other Jews in the town, was forced into a ghetto, and then transported to Auschwitz. His mother and youngest sister were sent to the gas chambers on arrival, but he and his father (and, it subsequently emerged, two of his sisters) survived the 'selections' and worked in the camp as slave labour. As the Soviets advanced towards Auschwitz, the inmates were moved back towards Germany, where his father died in appalling circumstances in a concentration camp a few weeks before the end of the war. Wiesel survived, and at first lived in France in a camp for Jewish survivors, but as a stateless person. There he studied, became a journalist and published his first book, *Night*, in 1960.

It is an autobiographical account of his experiences as a child and then in the death camps, and recounts the loss of his childhood faith in the harrowing conditions leading eventually to his beloved father's death. The best-known passage in the book is his account of some prisoners being hanged in one of the camps with the other prisoners forced to watch. One of the victims was a young boy, who, because he was light, did not die quickly but writhed in agony on the rope. One of the observers asked 'Where is God now?' to which Wiesel replied 'In that boy.'[13] In the book the meaning is ambiguous; it could describe his loss of faith as his belief in God died, or it could be seen, as many Christians have seen it, a symbol of God's own suffering in the world. In his memoirs *All Rivers Run to the Sea*, Wiesel himself gives an explanation:

> There is a passage in *Night* – recounting the hanging of a young Jewish boy – that has given rise to an interpretation bordering on blasphemy. The theorists of the idea that 'God is dead' have used my words unfairly as justification of their rejection of faith. But if Nietzsche could cry out to the old man in the forest that God is dead, the Jew in me cannot. I have never renounced my faith in God. I have risen against His justice, protested His silence and sometimes His absence, but my anger rises up within faith and not outside it. I admit that this is hardly an original position. It is part of Jewish tradition. But in these matters I have never sought originality. On the contrary, I have always aspired to follow in the footsteps of my father and those who went before him. Moreover, the texts cite many occasions when prophets and sages rebelled against the lack of divine interference in human affairs during times of persecution. Abraham and Moses, Jeremiah and Rebbe Levi-Yitzhak of Berdichev teach us that it is permissible for man to accuse God, provided it be done in the name of faith in God. If that hurts, so be it. Sometimes we must accept the pain of faith so as not to lose it. And if that

13 Elie Wiesel (2006) *Night*. London: Penguin, p.65.

> makes the tragedy of the believer more devastating than that of the non-believer, so be it. To proclaim one's faith within the barbed wire of Auschwitz may well represent a double tragedy, of the believer and his Creator alike.
>
> I will never cease to rebel against those who committed or permitted Auschwitz, including God. The questions I once asked myself about God's silence remain open. If they have an answer, I do not know it. More than that, I refuse to know it. But I maintain that the death of six million human beings poses a question to which no answer will ever be forthcoming.[14]

In the passage that follows those words in his memoirs he also discusses the question of God's suffering.

> My Talmudist master Rabbi Saul Lieberman has pointed out another way to look at it. One can – and must – love God. One can challenge Him and even be angry with Him, but one must also pity Him. 'Do you know which of all the characters in the Bible is most tragic?' he asked me. 'It is God, blessed be His name, God whose creatures so often disappoint and betray Him.' He showed me a passage of the Midrash dealing with the first civil war in Jewish history, provoked by a banal household quarrel: And God wept; His tears fell upon His people and His creation, as if to say, What have you done to my work?
>
> Perhaps God shed more tears in the time of Treblinka, Majdanek, and Auschwitz, and one may therefore invoke His name not only with indignation but also with sadness and compassion.[15]

God is there in the suffering victims of this world's disasters. He was there in the Holocaust; he was there in the tsunami; he was there in Haiti, not as the puppeteer pulling the strings, but

---

14 Elie Wiesel (1996) *All Rivers Run in the Sea: Memoirs*. London: Harper Collins, p.85.

15 Wiesel, *All Rivers Run to the Sea*, p.85.

in the victims who suffered, just as he was not there in Pilate or in Herod, but in the victim on the Cross at Golgotha. That is where we can find God, and that is where we can choose now to follow him, in seeking to ensure that nothing like the Holocaust can ever happen again, and in ensuring that our world is managed in such a way that there are realistic warning systems for tsunamis, and that buildings in earthquake areas can be built to resist possible tremors. We cannot push all the blame on God, even though in the Cross, Christians can see him accepting some of it; the responsibility for managing the world lies with us.

Perhaps the last word in this chapter, however, should be left to another Jew who experienced the Holocaust. Etty Hillesum was a young Dutch Jewish girl in the Second World War who, when deportations in Holland began in 1942, came forward and volunteered for the Westerbork concentration camp, there to help in the hospital and to share in the fate of her people. In 1943 she was shipped, in one of the usual mass transports, to Auschwitz, where she died on 30 November 1943. She kept a diary, which she threw out of the train on the way to Auschwitz. Remarkably, it was discovered and published some years after the war.

The theme of her diaries becomes increasingly religious, and many of the entries are prayers. Her God is someone to whom she makes promises, but of whom she expects nothing and asks for nothing.

> I shall try to help you, God, to stop my strength from ebbing away, though I cannot vouch for it in advance. But one thing is becoming increasingly clear to me: that You cannot help us, that we must help You help ourselves… Alas, there does not seem to be much You Yourself can do about our circumstances, about our lives. Neither do I hold You responsible. You cannot

help us, but we must help You and defend Your dwelling-place in us to the last.[16]

For further reading

Bentley Hart, David (2013) *The Experience of God*. London: Yale University Press.

Doctrine Commission of the Church of England (1987) *We Believe in God*. London: Church House Publishing.

Greenberg, Irving (2001) 'Cloud of Smoke Pillar of Fire. Judaism, Christianity and Modernity after the Holocaust' in Michael Morgan (ed.) (2001) *A Holocaust Reader*. Oxford: Oxford University Press, pp.102–14.

Hick, John (2010) *The New Frontier of Religion and Science*. Basingstoke: Palgrave Macmillan.

Hillesum, Etty (1999) *An Interrupted Life: The Diaries and Letters of Etty Hillesum 1941–1943*. London: Persephone Books.

Marsh, Henry (2014) *Do No Harm: Stories of Life, Death and Brain Surgery*. London: Weidenfeld and Nicholson.

Rees, Martin (2002) *Our Cosmic Habitat*. London: Weidenfeld and Nicholson.

Wiesel, Elie (1996) *All Rivers Run in the Sea: Memoirs*. London: Harper Collins.

Wiesel, Elie (2006) *Night*. London: Penguin.

16 Etty Hillesum (1999) *An Interrupted Life: The Diaries and Letters of Etty Hillesum 1941–1943*. London: Persephone Books, p.218.

4

JESUS OF NAZARETH

One of the more extraordinary things that happened to me in Westminster Abbey was to be asked at fairly short notice to join the then Receiver-General in taking the Foreign Secretary of China round the Abbey together with the Chinese Ambassador and various members of the Embassy staff. The Foreign Secretary, who spoke excellent English, suddenly asked me when we were in the Shrine of St Edward what the evidence was for thinking that Jesus ever really existed. I realised any answer I gave had to be intellectually coherent, so I pointed out that two non-Christian historians, Josephus and Tacitus, had mentioned Jesus well within a hundred years of his death, and that the Gospels were written during the lifetime of some who would have known Jesus when he was alive; the writers would not have made up a wholly fictional figure. Today no serious academic scholar would deny that Jesus existed, but I acknowledged that some of the details of the stories about him in the Gospels may not be historically accurate.

Contained within that latter part of my answer is one of the major questions about Jesus – which Jesus do we believe in? New Testament scholars have often talked about a distinction between the Jesus who lived in Palestine and who died at Calvary, normally described as 'the Jesus of History', and Jesus as the Church later perceived and understood him, normally described as 'the Christ of Faith'. But disentangling those two concepts is difficult, because even within the New Testament itself the process of interpretation was underway, and it is now impossible to get back to 'the Jesus of history' without trying to deconstruct some of that earlier interpretation.

The debates that have already been mentioned about the nature of the Gospels make that a difficult exercise. They were probably written at least thirty or more years after Jesus' death, they were not biographies in any sense that we would use the term now, the authors almost certainly did not personally know Jesus in his lifetime, and their books were written to provoke faith and discipleship rather than give accurate historical information. The Gospels tell us far more about how the authors and communities for whom they wrote perceived the lasting significance of Jesus than what would normally interest a biographer today. We have no idea what Jesus looked like, whether he was ever married or had children (although it seems unlikely) and even the stories of his birth are uncertain. Are they history or theological interpretation?

Only two of the Gospels have anything about Jesus' birth, Matthew and Luke, but because in many churches the whole celebration of Christmas has been taken over with children in mind, they are often not considered as adult stories. When I was a parish priest we had nativity plays every year, performed by groups of children in the church, where the stories from Matthew's and Luke's Gospels were always conflated, leaving the impression of a single nativity story primarily for children. In fact the purposes of Luke and Matthew were anything but child-like. These are both profoundly theological stories, designed to bring out the significance of the child Jesus according to the wider purposes of the two authors. It is worth spending some time on them, partly because they are so well known, but also because they illustrate the problem of historical event and later interpretation.

The Nativity according to Luke

To understand Luke's purpose we have to move on nearly seventy years after the birth of Jesus. It was put well by C.B. Caird, the author of the *Pelican Commentary on Luke*.

> On the night of what we would now call the 18th July in the year 64 AD a fire broke out in Rome, which burnt for a week and destroyed half the city. Rumour, spreading like the fire itself, laid the blame at the door of the Emperor Nero; and he, to divert suspicion from himself, looked for a scapegoat. His choice fell on the Christians, because, as Tacitus tells us in his account of the fire, they were already 'detested for their outrageous practices'. During the legal inquiries that followed, the Roman Government learnt for the first time to distinguish Christianity from Judaism. Hitherto, Christians had been officially regarded as a Jewish sect and therefore benefitted from the exceptional tolerance with which the Rome had treated the Jews since Julius Caesar… The fire of Rome led not merely to a grim persecution of the Church in that city, but to a permanent change of legal status for all Christians throughout the empire.[1]

Christians therefore thought that they had to explain themselves to the Roman authorities; they had to show what this religion that they followed was, and they had to show its origins. That was the task Luke set himself. Luke was clearly a well-educated man, with a good command of Greek. If he was a Gentile, then he had a very good knowledge of Judaism, but if he was a Jew

---

1 G.B. Caird (1963) *St Luke.* Pelican New Testament Commentaries. London: Penguin. For a fuller and more complex discussion about the purposes of the Gospel see C.F. Evans (2008) *Saint Luke.* London: SCM.

he was certainly well integrated into Gentile society. He wrote his Gospel for someone whom he described as 'most excellent Theophilus'. It sounds as though Theophilus was a high-ranking Greek figure in the Roman government, although others believe he might have been a Jew and yet others see the name, which means 'Friend of God', as simply standing for anyone who would be happy with such a description. Luke wrote to explain to him the figure of Jesus, portraying him as someone of nobility, grace and charm. Luke suggested he was able to reproduce those same qualities in the lives of his followers and enabled even the outcasts of society to rise to decency and dignity.

He tells Theophilus his sources were 'eyewitness and ministers of the word'. When it comes to eyewitnesses of the nativity there must have been very few around when Luke wrote his Gospel, because he was probably writing some 70 or 80 years after the birth of Jesus. So it was primarily from 'ministers of the word' that he got the birth stories. These were preachers' stories, stories that tried to explain some particular point about Jesus rather than give an accurate historical account in any twenty-first century sense. And of those stories Luke certainly gave Theophilus an orderly account.

In Chapter 1 he tells of the birth of John the Baptist, and in Chapter 2 he recounts the birth of Jesus, both in a fairly stylised form, with an angel appearing to say what was happening, and songs that were sung in celebration of the annunciations and then the birth. Those songs are regularly used in public worship now. The Magnificat, put by Luke into the mouth of Mary, and the Nunc Dimittis, said by Simeon, a righteous and devout man in Jerusalem at the time of the presentation of the infant Jesus in the Temple, are both sung regularly at Evensong throughout the Anglican Communion. The Benedictus, allegedly said at the time of John the Baptist's birth by his father Zechariah, is sung at Matins, and the beginning of the Gloria, according to Luke said by the heavenly host to the shepherds in the fields at Jesus' birth, is said or sung at the Eucharist. They are all taken from Luke's first two chapters. It is quite possible the Church was already using them liturgically when Luke wrote his Gospel, and he simply incorporated those texts into his nativity stories. The Magnificat bears a striking resemblance to the words sung by Samuel's mother at Samuel's birth in the Old Testament story (1 Samuel 2.1–10). There, and in the stories of Zechariah and Elizabeth, and in the story of Simeon and Anna in the Temple at the time of the presentation of the infant Jesus, the point is continually being made that this Jesus was the fulfilment of a long series of hopes and expectations on the part of the Jewish people. That point would not have been lost on Theophilus.

Luke also had at least two other purposes in his nativity story. Chapter 2 of his Gospel starts with words familiar to anyone who has been to a carol service: 'In those days a decree went out from Caesar Augustus that all the world should be enrolled. This was the first enrolment, when Quirinius was governor of Syria. And all went to be enrolled, each to his own city.' For the historian there are problems with those verses. While Quirinius did indeed carry out a census when he was Governor, Luke says that all these things happened in Herod's reign, yet in fact Herod had died ten years before that enrolment took place. Also it was not normally a requirement that people should go to the place from where their family came to be enrolled. However, Luke's purpose was more than trying simply to give a date; he was saying that even the actions of the Roman authorities were made part of God's purposes. The Romans on the whole believed that history was simply a record of things that happened with no particular plan or purpose behind them. Jews, by contrast, believed that God was at work in history, with his controlling hand extending even to the decisions of the Roman authorities. Perhaps such a view cannot be sustained in quite the same way now, but it was certainly part of Luke's purpose then.

The second additional purpose Luke had was to show that this Jesus identified with the poor, the humble and the outcast. That theme runs throughout his Gospel and is there in two of the most well-known features of his nativity account. For first, where was Jesus born? It is Luke who says that it was in a stable, because there was no room in the inn. Could there be any greater way of identifying with the outcast than that? Interestingly, Matthew says nothing about the inn or the stable. Secondly, Luke also says it was shepherds who first recognised the significance of this birth, people often looked down upon by the orthodox religious authorities because their occupation made it almost impossible strictly to follow religious observance.

So what were to become central themes of Luke's Gospel were there right from the very beginning in his birth narratives, most notably expressed in the words of the Magnificat 'he has raised up the humble and meek.' This is no children's story, but a symbolic prefiguring of all that Jesus was to do later in his life.

The Nativity according to Matthew

Matthew's account, like Luke's, takes up the first two chapters of his Gospel, but is much briefer than Luke's. If we discount the genealogy of Jesus, Matthew's story is told in 31 verses in all, while Luke's story takes 132 verses. So Luke's account is far more detailed, and in Matthew there is nothing about a stable or even an inn or any census. The implication of Matthew's Gospel is that Bethlehem was the home of Mary and Joseph. There is nothing about a choir of angels, or shepherds.

What Matthew does stress, more strongly than Luke, is the fact that Mary was a virgin when Jesus was born. Also it is only in Matthew that we read of the visit by the magi, or wise men, of any flight to Egypt or of a massacre of innocent children by Herod, an episode of which there is no other record in any other historical account of the period.

So the two Gospel stories, while they have some things in common, are very different. That reflects their purposes. Matthew was writing for those knowledgeable about the Jewish background, but he was probably writing after the destruction of Jerusalem and its Temple in the year 70 AD by the Romans. This created a wholly new situation for Judaism. With no Temple and therefore no place for the regular round of sacrifice that took place there, there was a conflict as to the real heir to the Jewish tradition. On the one hand there was the emerging practice of Jewish communities finding a new way of worshipping without the Temple; but on the other hand there were the Christians, who certainly had emerged from Judaism but who now also incorporated Gentile converts into their religion.

Matthew's Gospel was written against that background and, rather notoriously, Matthew includes some strongly anti-Jewish statements in his Gospel reflecting that more competitive relationship. That is why one notable feature of Matthew's Gospel more than any other Gospel writer is that he was concerned to show that Jesus was the fulfilment of Old Testament prophesies and Old Testament hopes. Ten times in his Gospel Matthew uses the phrase, 'This took place to fulfil what the Lord had spoken by the prophet', or something very similar, and five of those ten occasions occur in the first two chapters in his account of the nativity.

A good way of looking at what Matthew was trying to do in his nativity stories is to look at those Old Testament passages that he sees being fulfilled by this birth. Four in particular stand out.

The first comes from the book of the prophet Isaiah. Some 700 years before Jesus was born, Assyrian troops were massed on the Israeli border. The childless king of Israel was terrified that Jerusalem would be overrun, and that the sacred royal line of King David would come to an end with his own death. The prophet Isaiah was angry with the king at having so little faith in God's power, yet at the same time he wanted to reassure him. So he wrote, as Matthew translates:

> Look, the virgin shall conceive and bear a son, and they shall name him Emmanuel', which means, 'God is with us'. (Matthew 1.23; *cf.* Isaiah 7.14)

Contained in that is a problem of translation. Matthew wrote in Greek, so the quotation he gave was from the Greek version of the Old Testament, known as the Septuagint. In the original Hebrew the word translated 'virgin' simply meant 'young woman' and in the context of Isaiah's original prophecy 'the young woman' or 'virgin' is Israel herself. Isaiah is trying to reassure the King that the royal line would be continued. The point of the prophecy is clear; the Davidic line would be saved, and Israel would be saved by the grace and generosity of God. He would not abandon his people. Matthew saw that hope, which would have been familiar to any Jew, being fulfilled in Jesus.

The second Old Testament prophecy, from the Book of Micah, refers to the same political crisis. It speaks in terms of Zion, or what we would call Jerusalem, labouring in birth pangs and hoping for a saviour. The great hero of Judaism and creator of Jerusalem as the royal city was King David, who came from a Bethlehem family some five miles to the south of Jerusalem. Micah wrote:

> But you, O Bethlehem of Ephrathah, who are one of the little clans of Judah, from you shall come forth for me one who is to rule in Israel, whose origin is from of old, from ancient days. (Micah 5.2; *cf.* Matthew 2.6)

So Micah too is looking forward to the birth of a better king than the one in power at the time, and was hoping the next king would be another shepherd-like King David springing from the ancient Bethlehem clan. He was to be disappointed. Such a hope was to be unfulfilled in his lifetime, but the hope that Bethlehem would produce another Jewish saviour like King David had been fixed in Jewish consciousness.

The third Old Testament prophecy is from the prophet Hosea: 'out of Egypt I called my son' (Hosea 11.1; *cf.* Matthew 2.15). This refers back to the exodus of Israel from Egypt. Genesis tells the story of the tribes of Israel going to Egypt with the support of Joseph to escape a famine. Initially the Pharaoh, whose first minister was the Israelite Joseph, welcomed them. However, over generations they were turned into a slave people building the pyramids for Pharaohs. Salvation came when Moses led them out of Egypt into the promised land of Israel. The whole basis of the subsequent existence of Israel – and indeed even now – is seen by Jews to rest on God's faithfulness in calling them out of Egypt.

So in Matthew's account the infant Jesus, like the tribes of Israel, went to Egypt to escape a terrible situation, in his case the dreadful action attributed to Herod in the massacre of the innocents. Then, like Moses, he came back out of Egypt to lead his people to a promised land, which as far as Christians were concerned was not just a piece of territory, but the whole world, claimed for and ruled by Christ.

The fourth Old Testament prophecy comes from the sixth century before Christ. By then, Jerusalem had been destroyed, the people of Israel, the northern kingdom, were exiled to Assyria, and the people of Judah, the southern kingdom, to Babylon. En route, the deportees were collected at a place called Ramah a few miles to the north of Jerusalem in a sort of concentration camp where they were held before their long march into the Babylonian captivity. Ramah was the place, according to tradition, where Rachel, the mother of the Joseph tribes, was buried, and so the prophet Jeremiah laments this disaster: 'Thus says the Lord: A voice is heard in Ramah, lamentation and bitter weeping. Rachel is weeping for her children; she refuses to be comforted for her children, because they are no more (Jeremiah 31.15; cf. Matthew 2.18).' Matthew saw that being fulfilled in the massacre of the innocent children, although there is no other historical evidence to suggest that such a massacre actually took place. Matthew's main point is that King Herod is the new Pharaoh, enslaving and destroying God's new chosen people, and it was from this enslaving Pharaoh that Jesus was to redeem his people.

So we can see that four of the key elements in Matthew's story owe their origins to Old Testament prophecies: the virgin giving birth, Bethlehem as the place of his birth, the flight to and return from Egypt, and the massacre of the innocents by a wicked king. Matthew's point is clear. This Jesus will be the fulfilment of all of those prophecies in a new and different way. Whether today we think the Old Testament can be used in quite that way, with a meaning divorced from the original context in which it was written and applied to a completely different situation, is a moot point; I suspect many do not. But Matthew certainly thought so, and it moulded his story.

That is true even of the most well-known of Matthew's nativity stories, the coming of the magi or wise men. Who were they, and whom did they seek? They were Gentiles, not Jews, yet they came to see 'The King of the Jews'. Their presence was a foretaste of the whole message of Matthew's Gospel: what had previously been for the Jewish people alone was now for everyone. What Old Testament story would the visit by the magi have suggested to Matthew's original readers? The visit by the Queen of Sheba to Solomon, when she presented the king with gold and great quantities of spices…and then she and her servants went home to her own country (1 Kings 9.24 – 10.6). The parallel is even clearer if you read one of the rabbinic commentaries on that passage that would have been familiar to Matthew's readers. For there it was said that the Queen of Sheba was guided to Solomon by a star.[2] Matthew's point is obvious. This Jesus is not only the new Moses and the new David, but was the new Solomon as well, the builder of the Temple. And as Matthew says later in his Gospel, he is indeed greater even than Solomon.

This is what Matthew was doing in his nativity stories. He was not concerned to give an accurate historical account of what happened, as though he were a twenty-first century historian. Rather he wanted to show that this baby was no ordinary baby; and by interpreting Jesus against the background of the Old Testament he proclaimed that Jesus would usher in a new world, where the promise to the Jews would be extended to Gentiles as well. He was a new Moses, a new David, a new Solomon, and it was Gentiles who were the first to recognise it. Jesus was

---

2 H.J. Richards (1973) *The First Christmas: What Really Happened?* London: Mowbray, p.41.

the root from which all that was good in Judaism would be maintained in the world.

The birth of Jesus

So what are we to make of all of this? What significance can all of these stories have for us today? What is real history, and what is legend? Sadly, it is impossible to know the answer with anything like certainty, but we can note some real historical problems.

It is impossible for both Luke and Matthew to be right about what happened to Jesus straight after his birth. Matthew describes Jesus being taken to Egypt by Mary and Joseph straight away in order to escape the violence of Herod. Luke, who says nothing of the massacre of the innocents, has Jesus being presented in the Temple in Jerusalem, very shortly after his birth. They cannot both be right. It is also very difficult to be clear about when Jesus was born. Luke's attempt to date it to the census carried out by Quirinus when he was Governor would mean that the birth happened in about the year 6 or 7 AD, but Luke also says that Jesus was born during the reign of Herod, and Herod died in 4 BC, some ten years earlier. Trying to trace the story of the star guiding the magi by reference to the appearance of comets simply misunderstands the nature of its role in the story, which was to show, among other things, the similarity of this story to what had been said about the Queen of Sheba's visit to Solomon, following a star.

There is also a problem in what is sometimes described as the argument from silence. Matthew's and Luke's accounts both contain some remarkable elements: choirs of angels in Luke's case, and miraculously led visitors from the East in Matthew's case. There is agreement between the two that Jesus was born in Bethlehem, that Mary was a virgin and that the baby received visitors. Yet there is no reference to this in any other book of the New Testament. Neither Mark nor John says anything about Jesus' birth in their Gospels, and Paul makes no reference to it in his letters. It is at least odd that stories that appeared in writing late in the first century were not referred to at all earlier in the written Christian tradition – if, that is, the stories really happened as they are described.

This has led some biblical scholars to conclude that there is almost no historical element in these two accounts. Some would even go so far as to say that the whole Bethlehem tradition developed to make it seem that Jesus was the fulfilment of a particular prophecy. The editor of the *Oxford Companion of Christian Thought*, Professor Adrian Hastings, wrote the article on Jesus himself and says 'It seems likely that Jesus was born in Nazareth'.[3] Not all biblical scholars would be as definite as that, some certainly arguing that there is an element of history in the accounts of both Luke and Matthew, but what is certain is that among biblical scholars there is no consensus even on the place of Jesus' birth.

The scepticism of some would apply also to that most debated of questions: was this really a virgin birth, or, to be more accurate to the Gospels, a virginal conception? Some scholars say that the whole tradition of a virgin birth developed from Matthew's mistranslation, where the original text in the Hebrew 'young woman' was translated into Greek as 'virgin'. It is argued that Matthew believed that Jesus was the fulfilment of Old Testament prophesies, so if that was what the Old Testament said, he thought it must be true. If that was a mistranslation, which it certainly was, then that changes the matter. It is also

3 Adrian Hastings (2000) 'Jesus' in Adrian Hastings *et al.* (2000) *Oxford Companion to Christian Thought*. Oxford: Oxford University Press, p.340.

notable that the genealogies in both Matthew and Luke trace Jesus through the line of Joseph. Other scholars hold that deeper theological imperatives led to that belief, namely that Jesus was a deliberate act by God to bring about a wholly new situation in the world. Therefore, they would say, we should not be surprised that there is a miraculous element in the accounts of this birth, because the birth itself was miraculous in a far deeper sense than simply breaking the normal scientific explanations of things. It changed the world.

There are not very accurate statistics on who believes what, but the evidence appears to be that in the United States of America, belief in the virginal conception of Jesus is stronger in the general population than in this country. Some talk of 80 per cent of the adult population in America believing it as history, although a poll in 1998 showed that 44 per cent of American Episcopalian clergy doubt it. A survey of Anglican clergy in this country in the late 1990s found that just over 30 per cent of the clergy did not believe it was historically accurate. Truth, of course, cannot be decided on such a basis, but the figures are interesting.

Personally, I am not convinced that the historical veracity of the virgin birth matters very much, although scepticism makes me doubt it. There is a genuine scholarly debate, and has been for very many years. The 1938 Doctrine Commission report (discussed in Chapter 11) acknowledged that members of the Commission itself held varied views on it. Perhaps the most sensible thing is to consider that the gynaecological details of the birth of Jesus are not finally the point. What is undoubted, and incontrovertible, is that Jesus was born. When, where and how, is secondary to the fact of his birth. And, through his life and death, he did change the world. He fulfilled the purposes that Matthew wanted, because he made all that was good in

Judaism available to a far wider Gentile world, and he fulfilled the purposes Luke points to, because he identified with the poor and the outcast and raised them up to a new level of dignity. As the Magnificat sung allegedly by Mary at the annunciation put it:

> He has scattered the proud in the imagination of their hearts,
> he has put down the mighty from their thrones,
> and has exalted the humble and meek. (Luke 1.51b–2)

Because of Jesus the world is a very different place. His birth did change everything – and that is what finally matters.

The public ministry of Jesus

The stories of Jesus carrying out healing miracles in the Gospels are so numerous that it seems likely they were a significant part of what he did. How he did them is much more problematic. It would have been a common belief at the time that much illness was as a consequence of some sort of demonic possession. Jesus is certainly represented in the Gospels as practising exorcism, but few today would accept such a view of illness. Exorcism, however, could have gone hand in hand with other forms of 'faith-healing' indicated in the Gospel stories, which could simply be examples of changes effected by the faith of the healed person wanting change and induced by a particularly authoritative and commanding figure such as Jesus. Exactly what happened in individual cases is impossible to know. Many today also see the nature miracles, such as walking on water or stilling the storm, as exaggerations written up by convinced believers; but again the exact facts are unknown and unknowable. What these stories do show is the reverence and awe induced in those present, and in the Gospel authors, by the figure of Jesus. That may be what matters rather than any literal acceptance of the miracle stories simply as they stand.

But what of Jesus' teaching? The open-minded reader of the Gospels is confronted with an enigmatic figure who disturbs by his teaching. For today's reader of the Gospels, perhaps themost difficult part of his teaching was his apparent sense of the immanent end of the world. The parables he told about the Kingdom of God and a possible future judgement of the world can be read in the context of his belief that the world was about to end in some dramatic way in the near future. Whether that was really his meaning is much debated, with some seeing the judgement he spoke of being the immediate judgement his very being provoked, rather than something in the future. It is a complex debate that continues to this day, with no agreed resolution, and I shall discuss some aspects of that in the chapter on 'The Last Things'. But certainly he appears from the portraits painted by the Gospel writers as someone who provoked those who heard him to decide whether they were for or against him. It was impossible to be simply neutral.

Jesus expected people to trust in the reality of God as a force in their lives, and undoubtedly believed he was an agent of that God, and of something that he described as the Kingdom of God, which was both present and yet to come. His vision of God was of a loving and forgiving father, and that emphasis on forgiveness was a critical point of his teaching, the implications of which I discuss at greater length in Chapter 10.

In his teaching in general he appeared more concerned with the motives by which people acted than by whether they followed every detail of the Jewish law. In Galilee he spoke to large crowds of people who evidently found his teaching compelling. He used parables in a creative way to provoke the questions he thought confronted many in their lives, on which they were invited to make a judgement. In the process, he also attracted a group of close followers who implicitly trusted in him, and to whom he showed both love and judgement. The fact that he chose twelve was significant, since Israel was composed of twelve tribes, and Jesus seems to have realised that if his mission was to be continued it needed a group of followers who would carry on his work whatever happened to him. Whether he knew that going to Jerusalem would result in his death we cannot be sure, but it seems likely. He would have understood the political turmoil going on in Jerusalem at the time of the Passover, and would have known enough about the history of prophets to know that he was, at the very least, putting his life in danger by going there; yet he seemed to face that fact unflinchingly.

So why was he crucified? His summary of the law to love God and to love one's neighbour as oneself has a wide natural appeal; it is difficult to see why anyone should be deeply opposed to someone teaching that. What might have been more difficult for some of Jesus' contemporaries was his attitude to the Jewish ritual law. 'The Sabbath was made for man, not man for the Sabbath' would have been a challenging interpretation of the law for some of his more legalistically minded opponents. His sympathy for the poor and oppressed, together with his emphasis on the love and forgiveness of God, might also have alienated the more hard-hearted among the rich and powerful; but again it is difficult to see why it should have led to his final execution.

A clearer explanation comes in a book published in 1987 in England called *The Shadow of the Galilean*.[4] It is an unusual book of biblical scholarship in that it is immensely readable, even at times exciting! It was written by Gerd Theissen, professor

4 Gerd Theissen (1987) *The Shadow of the Galilean*. London: SCM Press.

of theology first in Copenhagen, then in Heidelberg. Theissen is known for his academic work on the politics, sociology and customs of Palestine at the time of Jesus, and he brought all that knowledge to bear on his book, which is a novel.

It concerns a wholly fictional character, Andreas, a wealthy Jewish merchant living at the time of Jesus in Sepphoris, the administrative capital of Galilee. The fact that Sepphoris is never actually mentioned in the Gospels shows that Jesus was essentially a man of the country rather than the towns. By a series of events, Andreas was forced into the role of being an informer for the Roman authorities, anxious to know what he could find out about the itinerant preacher Jesus. The Romans, like any occupying force needing intelligence and information, were concerned about Jesus because he was causing a stir. The novel is the story of Andreas trying to discover that information. In the process, Theissen sets Jesus very firmly in the context of first-century Palestine. He says he was 'most averse to write anything about Jesus that is not based on sources', and he goes on to say, 'There is nothing about Jesus in my book which I have not also taught at the university.'

Perhaps it is for that reason that Andreas only once saw Jesus, and that just after Jesus died on the cross. Theissen certainly does not make up stories of a living contact with Jesus, but instead reports what he has heard from a variety of people within Palestine. In the telling of that story Theissen conveys a wholly believable and realistic picture of the effect of Jesus on those who encountered him.

The book reveals a disturbed and often violent population, where many of the Jews lived fragile and unhappy lives against a background of political unrest and profound economic uncertainty. Although Andreas was typical of the wealthy Jewish merchants of Jesus' time, most of the Jewish population was poor, with little opportunity to escape the grinding poverty of their circumstances. Jesus is presented as essentially a man of the poor countryside rather than the wealthier towns, although some rich Jewish people supported him financially as an itinerant preacher. In particular, Theissen shows the deep divisions in that society and how Jesus fitted in to that context.

First of all, there was conflict between those who colluded with the Roman rule, like the ruling royal family of Herod Antipas in Galilee, and, to a lesser extent, some of the Temple authorities in Jerusalem, and those who rebelled against Roman rule and were, in our terminology, essentially terrorists. The Zealots were such a group and one of them, Simon the Zealot, became a disciple of Jesus. At one point in the novel, Andreas is captured by a Zealot group and becomes their prisoner until he manages to do a deal with them aided by one of the Zealot party, Barabbas, who in the novel was already known to Andreas.

In the conflict between those two groups Theissen shows clearly why the Roman authorities would be alarmed about Jesus. Whether the historical Jesus actually claimed to be the messiah is not clear. Mark's Gospel describes this as a sort of secret, suspected by some of Jesus' followers, but not a title that Jesus wanted to use in any public way. The one exception to that in Mark's account is at the trial before the High Priest, when Jesus is described as accepting the title of messiah. The historical accuracy of Mark's account of the trials of Jesus is debated amongst scholars, and it is difficult to be sure; but, as Rowan Williams has pointed out, for Mark, Jesus only accepts the title at the point when he is completely powerless before the Jewish and Roman authorities.[5] Williams argues that at that point only do we see the true nature of God's power, none

5 Rowan Williams (2014) *Meeting God in Mark*. London: SPCK, p.58f.

in the face of coercive force. But even if Jesus wanted radically to change the people's understanding of the nature of being messiah, he did attract messianic hopes, and such hopes would have been suspect to both the Roman and the Jewish authorities, particularly in the context of talk on 'the Kingdom of God'. Theissen stresses that Jesus' words about how Jewish leaders should treat people would have worried them, for Jesus was not concerned about forming a Church, but reforming Israel. The Roman authorities would have suspected a connection with the revolutionary policies of the Zealots.

But Theissen also shows why Jesus would have been unacceptable to the Zealots. His command, for example, to 'love your enemies' and 'to turn the other cheek' would have been very contrary to Zealot views on how to live in the face of Roman oppression. His ambiguous answer to the question about taxes, 'Render unto Caesar the things that are Caesar's, but to God the things that are God's', would also not have pleased a real Zealot, who would think downright opposition to all things Roman the only way for a true Jew to behave. In the novel, other Zealots perceive Simon the Zealot as being a traitor when he chose to follow Jesus.

A second area of conflict within Judaism concerned the Temple. On the one hand, the Essene community, living on the edge of the Dead Sea, believed the Temple was in the wrong hands, and so rejected the animal sacrifices of Temple worship and lived in their isolated community. What contact, if any, they had with John the Baptist is not known, but John worked in the wilderness, well away from the Temple, and proclaimed a baptism of repentance that did not require Temple sacrifices.

On the other hand, there were the Temple authorities, deeply committed to the blood sacrifices of animals in the Temple and seeing the Temple as the essential centre of Jewish religious life.

What was Jesus' attitude to the Temple? He submitted to John's baptism, itself in its way a public statement about what was and was not important in Jewish life, and he is reported as talking about the Temple being destroyed and rebuilt in three days, which the Temple authorities would have considered deeply subversive. He then caused uproar by overturning the tables of the money changers, thus challenging the whole structure of those in charge. But his complaint against the Temple was not that it existed, but that it was being misused; he spoke warmly of those who went to the Temple to pray in humility, asking for forgiveness. At the very least, Jesus was a radical reformer of the Temple practices.

So why was he crucified? We can be sure that if his death took place in the Passover period as the Gospel writers indicate, there would have been a vast number of extra people in Jerusalem and its environs at the time. In such a situation, with the possibility of heady nationalism stirring up rebellion, any Roman Governor would have been on his guard to put down anything that could cause trouble. A man from Galilee, speaking in a strange country accent and with a significant number of followers talking about a new kingdom would have been such a target. Jesus was probably perceived as a royal pretender, hence the sign that Pilate put on the cross, 'The King of the Jews'. His death would have been on the authority of Pilate, as only Romans had the power to order execution in that way, and other non-Christian historical sources tell us of Pilate's brutal reputation.

Although some of the Jewish leaders were perhaps complicit in Jesus' execution, the desire to blame the Jews more generally for the whole thing, clearly stated by Matthew and John, is probably a reflection of later Christian controversy between Church and synagogue, coupled with a desire to show the later Roman authorities who might read the Gospels that the burgeoning Christian Church had no basic quarrel with the all-powerful Roman Empire. As the American biblical scholar Robert W. Funk put it: 'That particular bit of Christian apologetic licence exercised by the earliest evangelists has deeply compromised Christian integrity for many centuries and led to atrocities beyond reckoning.'[6] But the essential fact is that Jesus met a horrible death at the hands of the Roman authorities, probably because they were concerned at the threat he posed to public order.

For further reading

C.F. Evans (2008) *Saint Luke.* London: SCM Press.

Adrian Hastings (2000) 'Jesus' in Adrian Hastings *et al.* (2000) *Oxford Companion to Christian Thought.* Oxford: Oxford University Press, pp. 340–2.

H.J. Richards (1973) *The First Christmas: What Really Happened.* London: Mowbray.

H.J. Richards (1975) *The Miracles of Jesus: What Really Happened.* London: Mowbray.

Gerd Theissen (1987) *The Shadow of the Galilean* London: SCM Press.

Rowan Williams (2014) *Meeting God in Mark.* London: SPCK.

6 I noted this many years ago but cannot now find the exact reference in Funk's works.

5

THE RESURRECTION

For his followers, Jesus' death must have been a disaster and a source of despondency and demoralisation. What seems to have changed them is the resurrection. But just what does that mean? The conviction central to the Christian Faith is that Jesus' death was not the end. All that he was and all that he stood for was not destroyed by the Cross, but somehow completed by it, and he remains a powerful force in the life of his followers today. But if that is what resurrection faith might mean now in terms of how a Christian person lives, what actually happened to bring about that belief?

The witness of the New Testament is that there were two things. First, when the women, Mary Magdalene and others, and then later two of the disciples including Peter, went to visit the tomb, they found it empty. Secondly, the Risen Christ appeared on a number of occasions to confirm that he had indeed conquered death. Seeing those two assertions as historically accurate has been the faith of many Christian people since the very earliest days, and among those who have written more recently on the resurrection is the former Bishop of Durham, Tom Wright, who asserts that it was only the combination of those two as actual historical facts that could account for the subsequent establishment and growth of the Church.

But anyone who is at all familiar with recent scholarly literature about the resurrection will know there has been great debate amongst biblical scholars about both those dimensions. That is partly because even in the Church there are some who are frankly sceptical about stories of bodies disappearing and the dead re-appearing. That does not apply to all Christians; many are clearly very willing to retain notions of the miraculous intervention by God into the details of history, but others, who have perhaps drunk more deeply from the well of scientific scepticism, at least retain a certain questioning approach about such matters. But there are also some genuine questions raised by a careful examination of the New Testament itself, questions I have always believed the Church should be open about, and which should not be simply confined to discussion in some academic closet.

Take the tradition of the empty tomb. The earliest evidence of the resurrection comes not from the Gospels but from Paul's letters, written some years before the Gospels were written. In particular, Paul wrote to the Corinthian church, where, from what he says, even then some questioned the resurrection. He was the only actual observer of the Risen Christ whose own account appears in the New Testament itself, and he describes his experience, although surprisingly briefly, in the letter to the Corinthians (1 Corinthians 15. 3–11) and also in his letter to the Galatians (Galatians 1.11–17). The accounts of his conversion in Chapters 9, 22 and 26 of the Acts of the Apostles were written many years after Paul's death.

In 1 Corinthians, Paul says that Jesus died and was buried, and then gives a list of various people to whom Christ appeared, but he says nothing about the nature of those appearances and when he describes the one to him it is surprisingly brief; 'Last of all, as to one untimely born, he appeared also to me.' In his letter to the Galatians it is even briefer: God 'was pleased to reveal his Son to me'. But even though in the Corinthian passage he is arguing for the resurrection, he says nothing about the tomb being found empty.

An argument from silence is always a difficult one, but some scholars, including Geoffrey Lampe (1912–80), Ely Professor of Divinity in Cambridge when I was there as an undergraduate, thought that silence so significant that he concluded the tradition of the empty tomb was not something that Paul knew, and that it was probably a later invention by the early Church. Other New Testament scholars share that view, believing the resurrection stories in the Gospels developed over the years when the Gospels were being written. This was not simply an expression of the radicalism of the 1960s; the 1938 Doctrine Commission Report also noted that some of their members believed 'the connection made in the New Testament between the emptiness of the tomb and the appearances of the Risen Lord belong rather to the sphere of religious symbolism than to that of historical fact'.[1] Other theologians and biblical scholars, including the Roman Catholic theologian Hans Küng, share such historical scepticism.[2] Indeed, some scholars even doubt whether the whole tradition of a particular identifiable tomb was historical, and that Jesus' body may have been thrown into a common burial pit with other criminals. The traditional site of Jesus' tomb in the Church of the Holy Sepulchre in Jerusalem was only identified as such in the fourth century.

---

1 Church of England Doctrine Commission (1938) *Doctrine in the Church of England*. London: SPCK, p.86 (For further details see Chapter 11).

2 Hans Küng (1978) *On Being a Christian*. Glasgow: Collins Fount Paperback, pp.343–81 (although more generally the whole of Chapters 5 and 6 of section C 'The Program' (pp.343–462) deal with wider issues of what belief in the resurrection and other parts of the Christian tradition mean.)

Peter Carnley, Archbishop of Perth and Primate of the Anglican Church in Australia until 2005, provides a useful and balanced examination of the evidence for the resurrection in a book published in 1987 called *The Structure of Resurrection Belief*.[3] He concluded there that the evidence for the empty tomb is ambiguous, neither strong enough to assert nor to deny that it was empty, a view he restated in a series of essays on the Resurrection published in 1998. It is not just unbelieving sceptics who wonder about the historicity of the empty tomb; even faithful and serious Christians like some of the members of the 1938 Commission on Doctrine (which I discuss in Chapter 11), and others such as Professors Lampe, Küng and Archbishop Carnley thought the matter an open question. Of course, other Christians, like Bishop Tom Wright, disagree with their conclusions.

That sort of debate applies to the second element in the resurrection, the appearances. The earliest accounts are again from the letters of Paul, but they simply say that Jesus appeared to various people, and give no details of what those appearances looked like. There is some disagreement in the three versions of Paul's conversion in the Acts of the Apostles on whether those with Paul heard the voice that spoke to him or not (Acts 9.3–19; Acts 2.6–21; Acts 26.12–18). Some have seen in those accounts, with the blindness and other physical consequences that followed, evidence of a sort of nervous breakdown, as it suddenly dawned on Paul that this group of people whom he was persecuting actually had the truth about God. What was also clear from those accounts is that it was a visionary experience and not any sort of physical contact with the risen Christ.

3 Peter Carnley (1987) *The Structure of Resurrection Belief*. Oxford: Clarendon.

When we turn to the Gospels, we find that each has a rather different account. The vast majority of biblical scholars believe the last chapter of the first Gospel to be written, Mark's, ends at verse 8, with the women fleeing from the tomb with trembling and astonishment, and with no original account of any resurrection appearance. Most scholars believe the rest of that chapter was a later addition, put in because of the oddness of Mark's Gospel ending at verse 8.

Matthew and Luke have rather different pictures. Matthew has Jesus appear to the women fleeing from the tomb, and asking them to tell the disciples to go to Galilee, and then Jesus appears to the disciples on the mountain in Galilee. But in Matthew's Gospel the accounts are very brief, only 20 verses in all.

Luke's Gospel has nothing about any appearance by Christ near the tomb, but according to Luke it was angels who gave the women the message that Jesus had risen. Luke then has accounts that appear only in his Gospel, the story of the disciples on the road to Emmaus, the disciples recounting that Jesus had appeared to Peter, and then Jesus appearing to all the disciples and departing from them at Bethany, near Jerusalem. Luke elaborates that story in the Acts of the Apostles with his account of the Ascension. In contrast to Matthew, Luke says nothing about any appearances in Galilee; all the appearances in his Gospel happen in or near Jerusalem.

It is only when we get to John's Gospel, which many scholars believe was a much later document, that we get the more detailed stories with which we are familiar: Jesus appearing to Mary Magdalene by the tomb, then to most of the disciples in Jerusalem, then to Thomas a week later, and then, in the final chapter, the various appearances in Galilee.

These very different accounts are problematic. It is difficult to square the appearances that Paul identifies to the Corinthians with the various accounts of appearances that occur in the different Gospels. The variety of the stories of appearances in the Gospels, with those Gospels that are widely believed to be later having more accounts of appearances than the earlier ones, also makes the objective reader wonder how much of those stories are actual history and how much are later reflections of the Gospel writers seeking to strengthen the belief of their readers in the resurrection. It is also notable that it is only in the later books of Matthew, Luke and John, all probably written forty or more years after the events they describe, that the resurrection body of Jesus appears to be of such a sort that he can be physically handled and is observed eating; Paul's account of the resurrection contains nothing like that.

There is also a problem of the consistency of the various Gospels. If one believes, for example, that John's stories are accurate, and that the appearance to Thomas in the presence of the disciples a week after the first Easter Sunday was historically the case, there is the extraordinary problem that neither Mark nor Matthew nor Luke mentions it. Why? Did they not know of it, or did they not think it important? Either explanation seems very remarkable, which is no doubt one of the reasons why a number of New Testament scholars doubt that story's historical accuracy as opposed to its theological value.

All these questions have led some scholars, particularly those associated with *The Jesus Seminar* in America, to think that all the resurrection stories were later creations of the Church. The resurrection for them was really the resurrection of Jesus in the life of the early Church. Personally, I doubt the evidence leads to quite such a negative conclusion, but in terms of what some Christians believe then it must be included as an option.

But if one believes, as I do, that some sort of appearances must have happened, what sort of appearances were they? Were they ones that, if cameras had existed at the time, would have been caught on film, or were they appearances given only to those who had the eyes of faith? If the latter, as seems at least possible from the limited evidence we have, then in what sense can we say they were real objective appearances rather than subjective visions, like the visions people do sometimes have of those who have died who were very important for them? Given the length of time between the events and their being written down in the Gospels, and then the passage of time until now, it seems very unlikely that we shall ever know for certain the answer to such speculation.

Those are the sorts of questions that lie behind the debates of New Testament scholars, and the important point is that there are serious Christian men and women on all sides of the argument.

One of the best defences of the traditional view is given by John Austin Baker, a former Canon of Westminster and then Bishop of Salisbury. His book *The Faith of a Christian* has an Appendix entitled 'The Nature of Jesus' Resurrection, and the evidence for it'. It is a detailed examination, and he certainly acknowledges various problems, although he strongly asserts the reality of the empty tomb. Of the appearances he says 'The amazing nuclear explosion of theological understanding of Jesus which we find in the New Testament within so short a time can be adequately explained only in one way: that it began from the eyewitness recollections of those post-Resurrection meetings of Jesus with his friends.'[4]

However, there are alternative views. We have noted Geoffrey Lampe's view on the tradition of the Empty Tomb, a view shared by Hans Küng and possibly Archbishop Carnley. Of the appearances Lampe wrote:

---

4 John Austin Baker (1996) *The Faith of a Christian.* London: Darton, Longman and Todd, p.199.

> The appearances recorded in the Gospels…are stylised, and the presence of Christ with his disciples is described in much more concrete, and at times materialistic, terms than in Paul's reticent allusions. Some of these…such as Luke's account of the journey to, and the supper at, Emmaus, are clearly reflections of, and meditations on, later Christian experience, cast in the form of an Easter story…Neither these stories nor those of the empty tomb can help us much in trying to answer the question whether the 'appearances' actually generated the conviction that Jesus had been vindicated and exalted, or whether they were visual and aural experiences resulting from, and expressive of, that belief. Still less does the New Testament evidence enable us to answer the question whether these appearances were subjective visions, or whether a personal, that is to say, a physical, presence of Jesus was actually seen with men's bodily eyes.[5]

Maurice Wiles comments on an earlier book by Baker *The Foolishness of God*, which essentially makes the same argument as in *The Faith of a Christian*:

> John Baker is much more confident than I feel able to be that the resurrection 'as an objective event' is to be included among those 'aspects of the story of Jesus of Nazareth' which can reasonably demand our assent to them as historical realities after a 'detailed historical critique' of the evidence.[6]

It may be relevant to note that Baker was a Bishop, while Lampe and Wiles were, by then, Regius Professors of Divinity, one at Cambridge and the other at Oxford. I hesitate to say this illustrates the 'psychological scepticism' I mentioned in Chapter 2, as I am quite sure all three were deeply honourable men. But what

---

5 Geoffrey Lampe (1977) *God as Spirit: The 1976 Bampton Lectures*. London: SCM Press, p.149.

6 Maurice Wiles (1974) *The Remaking of Christian Doctrine*. London: SCM Press, p.78.

someone's public role is must at least subconsciously influence what he or she believes and writes. I make no claim to be an academic, but it may not surprise the reader to know that my sympathies are more with the professors than with the bishop. The upshot is that there is a serious debate to be had about the resurrection; it is not a simple question of swallowing the lot or leaving it.

But perhaps even more important is that today a huge number of people belong to the worldwide Christian Church and find Jesus to be an inspiration that provides for them a guide on how to live. That is what *The Jesus Seminar* is pointing towards. Whatever it was that caused resurrection belief in the first place, for someone who held no official position and died an ignominious death that must indeed be resurrection.

For further reading

John Austin Baker (1970) *The Foolishness of God.* London: Darton, Longman and Todd.

John Austin Baker (1996) *The Faith of a Christian.* London: Darton, Longman and Todd.

Peter Carnley (1987) *The Structure of Resurrection Belief.* Oxford: Clarendon.

Hans Küng (1978) *On Being a Christian.* Glasgow: Collins Fount Paperback.

William Purcell (ed.) (1966) *The Resurrection: A Discussion Arising from Broadcasts by G W H Lampe and D M Mackinnon.* London: Mowbray.

H. J. Richards (1980) *The First Easter: What Really Happened?* Glasgow: Collins Fount Paperbacks.

N.T. Wright (2003) *The Resurrection of the Son of God.* London: SPCK.

6

THE CHRIST OF FAITH

The best biblical scholarship suggests that it is very unlikely Jesus of Nazareth considered himself to be God incarnate, or the second person of the Trinity. It is also unlikely that his earliest followers thought of him in these ways. They clearly thought he was a remarkable teacher and that he had some sort of divine mission that would bring about a new order in Israel. In the Old Testament the Book of Exodus refers to Israel itself as 'God's Son' and in Jewish literature the terms sons of God and Son of God are applied to the leaders of the people, kings and princes. By the use of that term they implied that the person concerned was an agent of God, acting in some way on his behalf. The earliest disciples certainly saw Jesus in that way, but what would have been far more difficult for any first-century Jew living wholly in a Jewish milieu would be to consider any human being as being God himself. They would have considered that blasphemous.

Changing that took time, although the experience of the resurrection, whatever that might have been, started the process. The Prologue of John's Gospel, so often read today at Christmas services, had its great influence: 'In the beginning was the Word, and the Word was with God, and the Word was God… The Word became flesh and dwelt among us, full of grace and truth (John 1.1,14).' That was a reflection on the life of Jesus, but was certainly not the only way of interpreting him. Most of the Gospel passages which say that Jesus was in some way God come from John's Gospel; the picture is far less clear in the Synoptic Gospels. If, as many scholars hold, John's Gospel is a late composition and the words attributed to Jesus there were not spoken by the historical Jesus of Nazareth, the argument adduced in some circles that 'Jesus claimed he was God. If so, he was either mad, bad or what he says he was' is based on the false supposition that Jesus claimed he was God. Certainly the early Church made that claim, but the truth of that does not turn on the personal integrity of the historical Jesus.

The relationship of the divine and the human in Jesus was a matter much debated in the life of the Church during the first four centuries, with various exponents stressing either the humanity or the divinity of Jesus, or some sort of combination of the two. Those arguments over the first four centuries were only more or less resolved at the Council of Chalcedon in the year 451. The Chalcedonian definition, signed by the bishops present at the Council, spoke of One Person in Two Natures, 'truly God and truly man…of one substance with the Father as touching the Godhead…of one substance with us as touching the manhood'. That seemed to resolve the problem politically, in that most, although not all, Bishops and churches were prepared to accept this definition. Whether it really resolved the theological question is more difficult to know. Some maintain that it simply restated the problem.

What is clear is that by the time of the Council of Chalcedon the Church had firmly moved from its original Jewish background into one far more influenced by Latin- and Greek-speaking cultures, and the whole philosophical way of thinking about God and man in those cultures was very different. In a wholly Jewish culture the notion that a man could also be God would have been very challenging to their normal way of thinking – as, indeed, it probably is now for most people in our own world. To the Greek mind, however, a figure so obviously close to God as was Jesus seemed clearly divine. Their problem would have been to see how he could also be human.

There is a very complex history of theological debate on that question in those first centuries, but a more modern take on that early history was made nearly 50 years ago by an American Professor of Theology, John Knox, in a book published in 1967, entitled *The Humanity and Divinity of Christ.*[1] The study of the relationship between the human and the divine in Jesus is known as Christology, and Knox traced what he called three ancient Christologies.

The very earliest followers of Jesus would quite naturally have accepted that, in his lifetime, whatever else Jesus was he was a man; an extraordinary and remarkable man certainly, but a man nonetheless. A very early understanding of Christology is expressed in the words of Peter, when after the day of Pentecost he says to the men of Israel, 'God has made him both Lord and Messiah, this Jesus whom you crucified' (Acts 2.36). To give it its technical title, this is known as Adoptionism. God in effect adopted Jesus through the resurrection to make him into a divine figure. As a matter of historical experience that must have been how it seemed to the disciples. They knew Jesus as a man; they had talked with him; they had eaten with him; they recognised him as a human being like themselves. They may have seen him as a remarkable teacher, but still as an essentially human figure, albeit one sent by God. It was only later, and especially after whatever it was that caused their belief in the resurrection, that they started to think of him as anything more than a man.

1 John Knox (1967) *The Humanity and Divinity of Christ.* Cambridge: Cambridge University Press.

Knox suggests that this way of looking at Jesus, as a human being who somehow became divine, could not last long in a world dominated by Latin and Greek thought, and it did not. A person of the first few centuries would not have seen this whole process as an accident of history; God must have planned it in some way. And if that was the case, the whole idea of Jesus as God's agent must have meant that, before he was born, he was at the very least an idea in the mind of God, which meant he must have existed before he was born. In other words, Jesus pre-existed as God before he became a man. So it followed that there must have been a moment of some sort of self-emptying of his divinity at his birth, an idea expressed in Paul's letter to the Philippians, where he says of Jesus, 'who, though he was in the form of God, did not regard equality with God as something to be exploited, but emptied himself, taking the form of a slave, being born in human likeness' (Philippians 2.6–7). There you have the second Christology, called Kenosis, the Greek word for emptying. It expresses the notion of a divine person who was with God from the very foundation of the world, who then emptied himself of his divinity to become fully man before resuming his divine status after the resurrection.

The third of the Christologies, which Knox believed developed in part of the Church later, is what is called Docetism, from the Greek word *dokein*, meaning 'to seem'. This view held that Jesus only seemed to be human, but in fact was divine all along. This was considered a heresy by the main part of the Church, especially when it was said that even his sufferings were not really felt by the divine person Jesus. That was deemed heretical, but it has to be said that in some popular Christianity even today there are strong Docetic elements, where some see Jesus as though he was God simply dressed up as a human being and not really a man like us. In that conception of Jesus he certainly did not share the human weaknesses and ignorance that seem to most of us to be an inherent part of our humanity.

However, Knox believed that ultimately neither of these latter two Christologies could work, for the simple reason that any notion of the pre-existence of Christ creates intolerable problems. How can any truly human being have been truly human if in fact he had already been God? The problem with these two Christologies of the Greek and Latin speaking worlds, Knox thought, lay in the notion of Jesus' pre-existence, a view shared by a number of other modern writers on the subject. I think they have a point.

Nonetheless the Church maintained the view that Jesus was the incarnation of God, and that God the Son was the second person of the Trinity. It was a position well argued for in contemporary terms by John Austin Baker in the books mentioned in the previous chapter. Where the belief of incarnation came from he outlines as follows:

> Jesus was a Jew. His faith was the Judaism of his day, radically reshaped in accordance with his own spiritual vision, but still Judaism; and there is no evidence that he planned to supersede it with another system of belief. What Jesus taught was in many respects very different from the faith which the rest of the New Testament proclaims, and certainly from developed Church Christianity.
>
> The reason for this is perfectly straightforward. The first Christians never claimed to be handing on a religion taught by Jesus. They were preaching a belief about Jesus and his central place in God's purpose. They did indeed draw some distinctive elements of their worship, practice and ethical conduct from the memories of Jesus and his teaching. But if anyone, in their minds, was the 'founder' of their particular 'Way', it was not Jesus but God the Holy Spirit. For it was by the inner light given

> to them, as they believed, by God himself that they had come to see Jesus as God's appointed Saviour, first to the Jews and then, through the Jews, of the whole world.[2]

It was that which led Baker to express his certainty in the Resurrection, on which I commented in the last chapter, and from that he argued that it led the early Church to the conviction expressed in the Prologue to John's Gospel that 'the Word was made flesh'. Jesus was seen not just as a man with a remarkable relationship with, and mission from God, but was the second person of the Trinity, God the Son, or God incarnate.

That came to be challenged in three books, all by significant figures in the world of academic theology, written in the 1970s. First came *The Remaking of Christian Doctrine* by Maurice Wiles, Regius Professor of Divinity at Oxford. It was originally a series of Hulsean Lectures in the University of Cambridge given in 1973 and published in 1974.

Wiles thought there was an inherent difficulty about thinking that God as we conceive him now could ever be seen as wholly represented in a human being. The contrast between the reason why there is anything at all in a possible multiverse and the source of transcendent claims upon us on the one hand, and a single historical human being on the other is so great that he wondered whether, although did not state definitely, the very notion was nonsense. He also thought the search for an accurate picture of Jesus from the Gospels, and distinguishing between what Jesus thought of himself and what others thought of him, was a much-contested matter in New Testament scholarship. 'There is an oddity…in affirming of a particular historical person that he is the embodiment of the divine and at the same time acknowledge that our knowledge about him in himself is at

2 John Austin Baker (1996) *The Faith of a Christian.* London: Darton, Longman and Todd, pp.45f.

every point tentative and uncertain.'[3] In addition he also did not consider it was essential for Jesus' role in showing us about God and bringing about salvation that he should have been literally the Incarnate Son of God. Baker argued that incarnational belief could only have come about because of the truth of the resurrection accounts. That belief lies behind Wiles's comment on Baker's view of the Resurrection quoted in the last chapter, and its development into the doctrine of the incarnation.

This is inevitably a brief summary of a long and complex argument, although Wiles made it within the admirable constraints of 146 pages and not too much technical language. It is a book well worth engaging with as a whole.

The second book, *God as Spirit* by Geoffrey Lampe, Regius Professor of Divinity at Cambridge, was also originally a series of lectures, but his were the Bampton ones in 1976 in the University of Oxford, published in 1977. Lampe focused on the suggestion that:

> the concept of the inspiration and indwelling of man by God as Spirit is particularly helpful in enabling us to speak of God's continuing creative relationship towards human persons and of his active presence in Jesus as the central and focal point within this relationship.[4]

He did not dismiss the possibility of incarnation, but rather widened it to include others.

> God has always been incarnate in his human creatures, forming their spirits from within and revealing himself in and through them; for although revelation comes from beyond the narrow confines of the human spirit and is not originated by man

---

3 Maurice Wiles (1974) *The Remaking of Christian Doctrine*. London: SCM Press, p.49.

4 Geoffrey Lampe (1977) *God as Spirit: The 1976 Bampton Lectures*. London: SCM Press, p.34.

> himself, there is not, and never has been, any revelation of God that has not been incarnated in, and mediated through, the thoughts and emotions of men and women. …In Jesus the incarnate presence of God evoked a full and constant response of the human spirit. This was not a different divine presence, but the same God the Spirit who moved and inspired other men, such as the prophets.[5]

Both Wiles and Lampe, in different but related ways, were questioning whether incarnation as a concept exclusively applied to Jesus was possible in the contemporary world, and whether it was fundamental to understandings of what Christ did, particularly through his death, of which I shall say more in the following chapter.

Their books were followed in 1977 by a group of academic theologians from English Universities producing a series of essays entitled *The Myth of God Incarnate*, edited by John Hick, Professor of Theology at Birmingham.[6] This also questioned whether the notion of incarnation as traditionally conceived was in fact essential for Christian Faith. The Preface to *The Myth of God Incarnate* quoted T.S. Eliot: 'Christianity is always adapting itself into something which can be believed.' The authors were convinced that the growing knowledge of Christian origins leads to the conclusion that Jesus was 'a man approved by God' for a special role within the divine purpose', but that later Christian conceptions of him as God incarnate, the second person of the Holy Trinity 'were a mythological or poetic way of expressing his significance for us'. They believed it was quite possible to hold that 'God was in Christ reconciling the world to himself' (2 Corinthians 5.19) without the traditional understanding of incarnation. Maurice Wiles was a contributor to the book,

---

5 Lampe, *God as Spirit*, p.23 f.

6 John Hick (ed.) (1977) *The Myth of God Incarnate*. London: SCM Press.

and in a chapter entitled 'Christianity without Incarnation' he wrote:

> The norm of Christian worship is an offering to God through Jesus Christ our Lord. The absence of incarnational belief would not simply destroy this mediatorial function altogether. It would still be possible to see Jesus not only as one who embodies a full response of man to God, but also as one who expresses and embodies the way of God towards men.[7]

The last chapter in the book was by Dennis Nineham, who was Geoffrey Lampe's predecessor as Regius Professor of Divinity at Cambridge. He asked:

> Is it necessary to 'believe in Jesus' in any sense beyond that which sees him as the main figure through which God launched men into a relationship with him so full and rich that, under various understandings and formulations of it, it has been, and continues to be, the salvation of a large proportion of the human race?[8]

The book provoked a major debate within the churches, including a rather negative discussion of it in the General Synod. But as Chapter 11 on Freedom of Thought in the Church of England shows, the Doctrine Commission never formally condemned the views of Wiles, Lampe and those of the authors of *The Myth of God Incarnate*. A diversity of views even on core theological matters is allowed within the Church of England.

The Doctrine Commission from 1981 decided to move to consider some fundamental Christian doctrines, with the first of a new series of studies being *We Believe in God* published

---

7 Maurice Wiles (1977) 'Christianity without Incarnation?' in John Hick (ed.), *The Myth of God Incarnate*. London: SCM Press, p.8.

8 Dennis Nineham (1977) 'Epilogue' in John Hick (ed.), *The Myth of God Incarnate*. London: SCM Press, p.202.

in 1987, and *We Believe in the Holy Spirit* published in 1991. Then in 1997 it produced *The Mystery of Salvation*, which I shall discuss in greater depth in the next chapter, but it returned to the matter of Christology in a most remarkable passage.

> The scandal of particularity is a non-negotiable part of Christian tradition. The whole point of the Judeao-Christian world-view is that the creator of the whole cosmos is in covenant with Israel; this was always ridiculous, seen in terms of the scale of near eastern empires, let alone in terms of the aeons of cosmic history. It always was something visible only to the eyes of faith. But to abandon it because it makes such an extraordinary claim is tantamount to abandoning the equally extraordinary claim that a first-century Jewish man executed by pagan authorities is the Lord of the entire cosmos. One cannot abandon the essential oddness of the particularity of God's choice of Israel – and of Jesus – without dismantling the very centre of Christianity.[9]

I believe you can abandon it without dismantling the very centre of Christianity if you allow that the perception of God's choice both of Israel and of Jesus is not something absolute, but rather a valuable and instructive metaphor. Interestingly later in the following chapter in *The Mystery of Salvation* the authors make extensive use of the notion of metaphor as applied to the sacrificial image of the atonement. I believe the same can be done to ideas of the incarnation and Jesus as God the Son. In any absolute terms they are possibly 'nonsense' (as in Wiles) or 'ridiculous' (as in *The Mystery of Salvation*), but they remain immensely valuable and helpful metaphors. Personally, I am content to continue to use them in that sense, and I suspect many contemporary Christians feel the same.

---

9 The Doctrine Commission of the Church of England (1995) *The Mystery of Salvation.* London: Church House Publishing, pp.79 f.

A more recent work on the subject of Jesus is by an Anglican priest, Stephen White, called *Jesus and the Christ* published in 2012.[10] He too argues against any notion of a pre-existent Jesus, or indeed of Jesus being God incarnate from his birth. Rather his basic contention is that Jesus was not born as Christ, but became the Christ through his life of obedience to God. At every point in Jesus' life, White believes that Jesus made choices and that matters could have gone another way. That they did not, and that Jesus remained faithful to his vision of God, is what made him the Christ. White argues that the Prologue to John's Gospel quoted earlier could easily be interpreted as meaning that it might have always been in God's mind to reveal himself to human kind. That was what 'the Word' meant in the Prologue; but when and how it happened depended on the right person making the right choices throughout his life. That Jesus did this can be a source of great rejoicing, not least of all because it was not inevitable. To my mind that interpretation gives a proper place to the free choices of Jesus during his lifetime.

Orthodox Christianity has always asserted Jesus was fully human, and I personally want that to be the starting point – as indeed it was for the first disciples. Whatever else Jesus was, he was a human being, with all the inevitable limitations that entails. But, by his life of faithful response to God, this man showed us something of God. When we look at Jesus, when we look at what he taught, when we look at what he did and see how he suffered, he does show us what God is like. He was, in the phrase used by Bishop John Robinson, the human face of God.

That does not mean that Jesus is God-like, as though we have some preconceived notion of God and then try to impose that on the human figure of Jesus. It is rather that God is Jesus-like;

10 Stephen White (2012) *Jesus and the Christ.* Dublin: The Columba Press.

the truly and completely human Jesus shows us what God is like. Did Jesus teach us profound truths about how to respond to God in the extraordinary opportunities and challenges life throws at us? Yes, he certainly did. Did he show us that God was loving and forgiving, and did he demonstrate this in his own being? Yes, he certainly did. And in his suffering on the Cross can we gain some insight into what it must be like to be God, suffering because of his love for a world that so often ignores and even seeks to destroy him? Yes, we can.[11]

This fully human Jesus shows us what God is like. In that sense, Chalcedon was correct, he was fully man according to his humanity, but fully God according to his divinity. Whether we can describe it today as two natures in one person is more problematic, because it is difficult if not impossible to conceive how one person, presumably with one consciousness, can have two natures in quite that way. But God was in Christ, reconciling the world to himself, as Paul put it, because he reconciles each of us to himself if we allow him to do so. That is what lies at the heart of the Christian belief in this fully human being.

A further dimension to this lies in the Christian doctrine of the Trinity.[12] The fully developed notion of God as Trinity took some time to emerge, although the seeds of it can be found in Matthew's Gospel, where the Risen Christ is reported as telling his disciples to 'make disciples of all nations' and to baptise 'in the name of the Father and of the Son and of the Holy Spirit'. Many scholars think these words are very unlikely to have come from Jesus himself, for three reasons. First, because this is the only occasion in the Gospels when Jesus is described as encouraging his disciples to baptise; secondly, because, according to the Acts

11 Further discussion of this can be found in Wesley Carr (1992) *Tested by the Cross*. London: Fount.

12 Matthew 28 v.19.

of the Apostles, the apostles baptised 'in the name of Jesus'; and thirdly, because nowhere in the rest of the Gospels did Jesus encourage his disciples to preach to the Gentiles – the Gentile mission came from Peter and Paul. The Trinitarian formulation in Matthew is very probably a later addition to the Gospel, perhaps even by a scribe who was simply reflecting the much later practice of the Church.

But the notion of God as Trinity caught on. There are not two persons in the one Godhead, but three. In addition to God, who is that very foundation of all that is, there is Jesus who shows us what God is like, and there is also God as he is experienced in and through the life of the world, often mediated through the influence of other people. Those who believe in God are influenced by that belief and express it sometimes in remarkable ways in their lives, which makes a difference to what happens. In that sense at least God is active in the world. The notion of the Trinity therefore becomes a way of describing the different ways in which God can be encountered. Far from being something obscure and theologically technical, the notion of God as Trinity is a simple explanation of the different ways anyone might encounter God. But it was a reflection of later Christian experience, and almost certainly not part of the very earliest Christian teaching.

Harry Williams provided a further dimension to the notion in an address he gave one Trinity Sunday in Trinity College Chapel in Cambridge. He suggested that human beings have two basic fears, one of being finally alone and deserted, and another of being somehow absorbed in a way that means individuality is subsumed. By suggesting that God contains within himself three individual persons in relationship with one another, the Christian Church was asserting that, in what might be seen as ultimate reality, neither isolation nor absorption has the final word. It was an interesting psychological perspective on what belief in the Trinity might also be about. But it also shows that Christian theology can never rest in one place. It will continually adapt to contemporary thought.

For further reading

John Austin Baker (1996) *The Faith of a Christian*. London: Darton, Longman and Todd.

Wesley Carr (1992) *Tested by the Cross*. London: Fount.

John Hick (ed.) (1977) *The Myth of God Incarnate*. London: SCM Press.

J. L. Houlden (1992) *Jesus: A Question of Identity*. London: SPCK.

John Knox (1967) *The Humanity and Divinity of Christ.* Cambridge: Cambridge University Press.

Geoffrey Lampe (1977) *God as Spirit*. London: SCM Press.

Geza Vermes (2000) *The Changing Faces of Jesus*. London: Penguin.

Maurice Wiles (1974) *The Re-making of Christian Doctrine*. London: SCM Press.

Stephen White (2012) *Jesus and the Christ*. Dublin: The Columba Press.

7

SALVATION

The Church has always spoken of Jesus as the Saviour. The implication is that through him salvation is offered. But what does that mean? In his article on 'Salvation' in the *Oxford Companion to Christian Thought* Adrian Hastings concluded 'Few words proper to Christianity's core vocabulary have at present a less defined meaning.' He was right, which is probably the reason I found this the most difficult chapter to write. What do we need to be saved from? A variety of answers have been given throughout the history of the Church. The Doctrine Commission Report mentioned in the last chapter, *The Mystery of Salvation,* puts the questions clearly.

> Is salvation going to heaven when we die or something experienced here and now? Is it deliverance from guilt and the threat of divine punishment or from the transience and mortality of earthly forces or from demonic forces which tyrannise over human life or from oppressive political and economic conditions? Is it a matter of knowing God or of living a better life? Is it the salvation of individual souls from a corrupt world or the creation of an alternative society in contrast to the world or a means of transforming society into the Kingdom of God? Does it make people divine or truly human?[1]

---

1 Doctrine Commission of the Church of England (1995) *The Mystery of Salvation.* London: Church House Publishing, p.28.

It goes on to suggest that these could be false alternatives; salvation might be both. But the report does distinguish between 'secular self-fulfilment' and Christian salvation in that the first is specifically not concerned with any notion of God while the latter is.[2] Perhaps it is best to start from the New Testament.

Paul, particularly in his letter to the Romans, said that salvation is from the eternal consequences of sin – 'the wages of sin is death' – and that Jesus' death was in some way an atoning sacrifice that made the offer and the acceptance of forgiveness possible. No doubt that reflected the need of the earliest Christians to find some interpretation of the devastating fact of Jesus' execution, and they used the most obvious language open to them, that of Jewish notions of sacrifice that took away the consequences of sin. Whether that makes sense in the contemporary world is less clear, for it raises at least five problems.

The first is a simple matter of language; how is the notion of sin understood today? If the word is used at all in popular speech, it is often seen to relate to minor peccadilloes – 'it is illegal, it's immoral, or it makes you fat!' – rather than to some deep-seated and profound rebellion against morality and God. More careful thought might lead many to recognise that, in practice, they have, at least at times, a sense of alienation from others, they do not always act unselfishly, and that human beings seem to have a capacity to make life difficult for one another. But most people are probably not weighed down by a massive sense of personal guilt and wickedness. Perhaps a few should be, but they are almost certainly a small minority. In my experience, many people, even though they acknowledge that from time to time that they have said or done things they regret, try to act honourably and honestly. Seeking to ferment a sense of guilt in them for their sin in order to create some sort of

2 Doctrine Commission, *Mystery of Salvation*, pp.34–6.

need for salvation does not seem to be a particularly helpful or even sensible thing to do. Of course, there remain some people who are burdened with a deep sense of guilt, but the solution to that is probably to be found as much from psychological help as from any theological insight.

A second problem is the relationship of the individual to the corporate. I am caught up in a network of relationships – with family, with local community, with national life – and in all of those areas there are corporate decisions to which I am inextricably bound, even though I may be personally concerned about some of them. Any democratic decision, whether made locally, nationally or internationally, often contains an element of self-centredness. For example, personally I am pleased there is a ring-fenced contribution for government spending on aid to the third world. Whether that should be 0.7 per cent of the Gross National Product or 0.71 per cent is a technical question, but whether it should be that or a far larger percentage is a moral question. I am uneasy about the low figure even if it does meet a UN target, but if a government in this country made a decision to increase it dramatically that might be very unlikely to receive democratic approval. Also, it would not have a really significant effect on world poverty unless it was a commitment shared by all other relatively wealthy nations. Responsibility for the ills of the world can never simply be laid at the door of individuals, so any realistic salvation must be wider in scope than that.

That relates to a third problem; who is saved? Paul, and some of those who follow him, certainly at times imply that each individual has to make a decision to receive the forgiveness offered by God and to follow Christ and at that point that individual receives, at least partially, salvation. But if salvation is simply limited to individual Christians then how far is it really salvation rather than a selfish preoccupation for the individual? Of course, in parts of the New Testament the scope of salvation is far wider than that. In John's Gospel John did not say 'God so loved the *Church* that he gave his only Son' but rather 'God so loved the *world*...' (John 3.16) A tension about the scope of salvation has certainly been recognised in much of the Church's subsequent discussion, so a broader view of salvation than simply something for Christian believers does appear fundamental.

A fourth problem about Paul's view is whether human beings need something as dreadful as the crucifixion of an innocent man to enable them to be forgiven by God. The solution seems disproportionate to all except the most heinous of crimes. The story is told of someone with particular evangelistic fervour trying to convert a friend by saying 'Don't you know that you were bought with a price', to which the friend replied 'I did not realise I was up for sale!' He had a point. Perhaps more common today in popular thought about forgiveness would be the comment of the German poet Heinrich Heine: 'God will forgive me. It's his job.' The notion that God is a merciful and forgiving God is fundamental to all the Abrahamic Faiths, even if they do not always live up to that as clearly as they might. The image of the cross as a sacrifice required by God to enable him to forgive appears at least doubtful and to some positively immoral. Personally, I find that quasi-juridical model of salvation profoundly unhelpful.

A fifth problem I shall discuss further in the next chapter, but if salvation is about hope for the future for the individual, how does someone who is frankly sceptical about any notion of individual afterlife make sense of that? Must that hope for the future include some personal hope for the individual believer?

So to come back to the fundamental question, what do we need to be saved from?

No one needs to look for long at the life of the world to realise that all is not well. Mistrust and conflict abound, both between individuals and between communities, and, if the human causes of what is wrong were not enough, there are also dreadful natural disasters. It could be said that, if salvation is needed, it is from being perplexed and depressed by the state of the world. We need a mental framework against which we can make sense of the world and then find a realistic way of having some hope to make things better. No one can suggest that is easy, but what can a thoughtful Christianity contribute towards such a search? It will have both an individual and a corporate dimension.

At the individual level the beginning of such a framework for me can be found in some words the German-American theologian, Paul Tillich, wrote over 60 years ago and which were quoted by John Robinson in *Honest to God.*

> Sometimes…a wave of light breaks into our darkness, and it is as though a voice were saying: 'You are accepted. *You are accepted…* by that which is greater than you, and the name of which you do not know. Do not ask for the name now; perhaps you will find it later. Do not try to do anything now; perhaps you will later do much. Do not seek for anything; do not perform anything; do not intend anything. *Simply accept the fact that you are accepted!*[3]

That sense of being accepted may provide a profound start for the individual, it does for me, but salvation cannot rest there. It must move to something more corporate and comprehensive. Yet if it is to be related to the Christian Gospel, it must also centre on the life, and perhaps especially the death, of Jesus. How can that work?

One of the changes to Christian thought about God in the last century is that it had to come to terms with huge levels of human suffering, as I discussed in Chapter 3. The notion

3 John A.T. Robinson (1963) *Honest to God.* London: SCM Press, p.81.

that God was somehow impassive and above such matters, which was more a Greek philosophical view than a Jewish one, simply became unsustainable. The point was vividly made by a First World War Army Chaplain, Geoffrey Studdert Kennedy (1883–1929), in one of the dialect poems he wrote for the troops. He was looking at the body of a young corporal who had just been killed, and wrote:

And the lovin' God 'E looks down on it all,
On the blood and the mud and the smell.
O God, if it's true, 'ow I pities you,
For ye must be livin' i' 'ell.
You must be livin' i' 'ell all day,
And livin' i' 'ell all night.
I'd rather be dead, wiv a 'ole through my 'ead,
I would, by a damn long sight,
Than be livin wi' you on your 'eavenly throne,
Looking down on your bloody 'eap
That were once a boy full o' life and joy,
And 'earin' 'his mother weep.
The sorrows o' God must be 'ard to bear
If 'E really 'as Love in 'is 'eart,
And the 'ardest part I' the world to play
Must surely be God's part.[4]

There is a long-standing tradition within Christian theology of looking at the death of Jesus as the pre-eminent example of God's passionate yet suffering involvement in the world. The French medieval theologian Peter Abelard (d. 1142) was a well-known exponent of what is sometimes described as an exemplarist view. The Cross is a particular and powerful example of something that continues to happen all the time.

---

4 G.A. Studdert Kennedy (2006) *The Unutterable Beauty: The Collected Poetry of G.A. Studdert Kennedy.* Liskeard: Diggory Press, p.130 f.

Wherever human flourishing is limited, or destroyed, or denied, God himself suffers. When John Robinson described Jesus as 'the human face of God', then perhaps in the death of Jesus we can see what happens to God when evil and injustice prevail. The idea was well expressed in the poem by Sydney Carter when he put into the mouth of one of those crucified with Jesus:

It's God they ought to crucify,
instead of you and me,
I said to the carpenter
a'hanging on the tree.[5]

Dietrich Bonhoeffer (1906–45), executed on Hitler's orders just before the end of the war, wrote shortly before he died that 'only a suffering God can help', yet that is what Christianity is pointing towards. For a long time, the notion that God suffered in this world would have been considered a heresy in the Church, but after the horrors of the twentieth century, starting with the response to the trench warfare of the First World War, it became less clear that was so wrong. God is eternally suffering in the victims of this world's disorders, and to approach the conflicts of our world in such a way may itself start to make a difference at least to our perceptions.

To see the Cross of Christ in that light is therefore a start. The God revealed in Jesus Christ shares our anguish at the state of the world. His power is not that of an absolute monarch, but rather the power of love. Love, care for others and compassion do not have absolute power, but they can and do make a great difference.

One of the other images that has been used in the Church over many years for making sense of salvation is seeing Jesus' life and death as a victory. It was originally presented as a

5 Friday Morning Chorus by Sydney Carter.

victory over the devil, which may not make much sense in our contemporary society, but it can also be seen as a victory over self-centredness and over desperate evil. Certainly during his lifetime Jesus is presented as doing that in the Gospels, but in all the Gospels he is presented as facing the dreadful agony of Calvary without his faith being destroyed. Both Matthew and Mark record his last words as being 'My God, my God, why hast thou forsaken me?', which may seem faith destroyed, but it is the opening verse of Psalm 22, as Jesus would certainly have known. Much of that psalm seems relevant to what happened to Jesus then:

I am poured out like water,
and all my bones are out of joint;
my heart is like wax;
it is melted within my breast;
my mouth is dried up like a potsherd,
and my tongue sticks to my jaws;
you lay me in the dust of death.

For dogs are all around me;
a company of evildoers encircles me.
My hands and feet have shrivelled;
I can count all my bones.
They stare and gloat over me;
they divide my clothes among themselves,
and for my clothing they cast lots. (Psalm 22.14–18)

But the psalm ends with a message of hope:

Posterity will serve him;
future generations will be told about the Lord,
and proclaim his deliverance to a people yet unborn,
saying that he has done it. (Psalm 22.30–1)

That may be why Luke could describe Jesus' last words as 'Into thy hands I commit my spirit' (Luke 23.46). I do not think it is misplaced to think that Jesus survived even the horror of the Cross with his faith in God intact. That was a great victory.

But the Christian Faith also asserts that the death of Jesus was not the end. As I outlined in Chapter 5, the details of whatever it was that caused the early Church to conclude that Jesus rose from the dead may be debatable, but the consequence is undeniable. Today a huge number of Christians throughout the world believe that all that Jesus was and all that he stood for was not ended by his death, but is still alive and is still changing things through the power of love. Many people respond to the anguish of the world by saying it cannot simply be the last word. They strive to change things so that anguish can begin to be overcome. A frequent yet profound example of that is when parents who have lost a child establish some charity in the child's name to respond to whatever it was that brought about the child's death. The desire to find something that can in its way be resurrection is very deep.

That desire is not an exclusively Christian phenomenon. Men and women of all faiths and none try to do that; it is a human response. But the Christian sees it as an example of salvation. That the Church calls the Friday on which Christ died Good Friday illustrates the point. Even the worst of things can be used to create something good. That can provide hope and inspiration to work for salvation. Salvation cannot just be something we receive as a gift, although I certainly believe it is that, but it must also the motivating force for seeking positive change. It is both a hope and a call for action. The image of death followed by resurrection does provide a story by which we can live our lives. It is not just a salvation that is personal to the individual, it provides a hope that is shared with others and can be the basis for active action and involvement in the world.

And it is a call that has been heard and responded to. Above the Great West Door of Westminster Abbey there are ten statues of twentieth-century martyrs, men and women who gave their lives for what they believed was right and Christian. Many visitors to the Abbey pause before them and no doubt in some cases find out more about them. But there could be many more than ten. While martyrdom in its most extreme form of physically being killed for your faith is relatively rare, there are many who give sacrificially for the sake of others in lesser ways and in the process make their contribution to the salvation of the world. Of course, salvation is not complete; I doubt it ever will be. But there will always be a need for those who, rather than just fulfilling their own needs, give of themselves in some sacrificial way to overcome tragedy or injustice. The hope that such things can be transformed is not misplaced, because Calvary shows that it can happen. That vision is salvation.

For further reading

The Doctrine Commission of the Church of England (1995) *The Mystery of Salvation.* London: Church House Publishing.

G. A. Studdert Kennedy (2006), *The Unutterable Beauty: The Collected Poetry of G. A. Studdert Kennedy.* Liskeard: Diggory Press.

Paul Tillich (1962) *The Shaking of the Foundations.* London: Pelican Books.

8

THE LAST THINGS

There are probably few areas of traditional Christian theology more difficult for many people today than what the Church has taught about the 'last things'. These will include the last things in a personal sense, death and whatever might happen beyond it for the individual, and also in a corporate sense, what might be meant by judgement at the end of the world. Perhaps it is best to start with the bigger picture.

The consummation of all things

There is much in the New Testament about the return of Jesus Christ, the end of the world and of judgement. The whole subject was later given the title 'eschatology', which dealt with the four last things: death, judgement, hell and heaven. The fundamental belief that underlies it is the notion that there is a narrative for the universe as a whole, which has a beginning and an end, and that in the end God will complete and finish his purposes. It was the theological pressure to find such a meta-narrative that led to a more developed notion of the last things, and such reflections were normally rooted in ideas of God. At its most fundamental, the picture was that at the end of time all would be raised from the dead, and then comes the judgement, when those responsible for evil would be punished and those who suffered for the good would be vindicated. It is an impressive vision, although insofar as it presumes to say what will happen in the ultimate future it can only be speculative. Such a view inevitably raises the question, 'Is it true?'

In one sense, that is a less contentious issue for most people than what happens to the individual after death, simply because many churchgoers probably ignore those eschatological passages, finding them slightly odd, hard to understand, but not immediately relevant to their lives. Of course, the question of the end of the world or at least of humanity is not in any way irrelevant. It might happen through some nuclear confrontation, or some dramatic disease for which there seems to be no cure, or massive and irreversible climate change, or even from some encounter with an asteroid of a type that distinguished scientists a few years ago concluded led to the extinction of the dinosaurs. But most people probably think that if such a cataclysm happens there is not much they can do about it. They can only hope either that action can be taken to stop any such disaster or, more selfishly, that such disasters will not happen in their lifetime or of those they know and care for. That at least does not seem an unreasonable hope, except arguably in the area of climate change for younger people. Probably most people do not to worry too much about the end of the world.

But anyone who wants to take the Christian tradition seriously must make some assessment of the eschatological and apocalyptic elements in the New Testament. The notion of judgement occurs in a number of the parables that Jesus told, and the more explicitly apocalyptic elements predicting the end of the world occur primarily in Mark 13 and the parallels in Matthew and Luke (but not, interestingly, in John's Gospel). They are also referred to in some of the epistles and, most notably, in the last book of the Bible, the Revelation to John.

The essence of apocalyptic writings about a coming disaster is that they reveal some hidden truth about what might happen through visions or dreams.

Revelation gives a strange and disturbing picture of the end of time. No one knows who the author of that particular book was. It has a style very different from any other books linked to the various Johns who occur in the New Testament. It seems possible it was written in a time of persecution of the Church by the Roman authorities towards the end of the first century and was intended to give encouragement to those who were facing such a difficult situation. That might provide a clue to the nature of apocalyptic writing; it was often prompted by extreme situations. It might well show what gave encouragement in those circumstances to the communities for which they were written, and to what they ultimately hoped for. But despite some Christians finding Revelation a happy hunting ground for references to interpret near contemporary events, this book does not give any information to us about today or for what might happen in our future. Such speculation completely misunderstands the nature of Revelation, which was to give vision and hope to those suffering at the time.

Reflections on eschatology have continued in various ways throughout the history of the Church, and a wholly different approach was provided by the French Jesuit priest and palaeontologist Teilhard de Chardin (1881–1955) in the first half of the twentieth century. He believed that evolution was not simply something that happened in the past, but that there is an evolutionary pressure from the future, drawing human kind and the world to something he described as 'The Omega Point', which was a final point of complexity and consciousness where God's purposes for human kind would be fulfilled. He was silenced at various times by the Catholic Church, mainly because it was held that he did not take a serious enough approach to the reality of human frailty and sin. More recently Pope Benedict showed a more sympathetic approach to his teachings and certainly said they should be carefully studied. However, it is very difficult to look at the world as we know it today and to conceive that it is naturally moving to a very positive conclusion.

What of the belief that Jesus would return again after his resurrection and be the agent of some final judgement? That was certainly there in some of the Gospels and the epistles. It became more muted in later books, however, and is hardly present at all in John's Gospel, where any future coming of Jesus is seen as fulfilled through the giving of 'the Comforter', the author's name for what was more usually described as the Holy Spirit. There remains an interesting question of where and how the whole eschatological theme developed in the Church. Whether the belief in any return of Jesus came from things Jesus had said about himself, or whether they emerged from a misinterpretation of things that he said, was the source of much debate in the nineteenth and twentieth centuries. The context was what Jesus really meant by 'the Kingdom of God'. Did he mean an end of the world, or an immanent kingdom that would come into being as a direct result of his life and death, or was it in fact a 'spiritual' kingdom already present in the hearts and minds of those who sought God if only they had the eyes to see it? The Gospels can be read in each of those ways – and have been.

One way of understanding the Kingdom was provided by a twentieth-century biblical scholar, C.H. Dodd, who in the 1930s talked about 'realised' eschatology. He considered that Jesus was not particularly concerned about the future, but did believe that through his life and death the Kingdom was brought into being. Jesus' parables of the Kingdom showed how that power was exercised in practice. Similarly, judgement was not something that would simply occur at the end of time, but something that is already present. The question for the Christian man or woman is whether they live as though they are in that Kingdom and under that judgement, so that their lives are governed by it. Some would argue that the theme of John's Gospel was such a 'realised' eschatology.

Personally, I find that the only way of making sense of the notion of judgement in the New Testament. Judgement is not some possible event in the future, but here and now for those who seek to live their lives in a Christian manner. Many can point to moments in their lives when they were aware of 'being judged', even if it was only in their own minds. The apocalyptic writings point to the values that their writers believed were ultimate: the final vindication of what God desired for the world. But seeking that requires taking the current life of the world very seriously indeed, and the judgement to which we are all open is about the choices we make as we live our lives now. Do we, in the words of the prophet Micah, seek to 'do justly, love mercy and walk humbly with God'? That challenge contains serious and disturbing questions on how we live our lives, and that might be enough in our contemporary age.

I suspect biblical passages are an unreliable guide to what might happen in our future. I see no evidence for thinking the authors of the New Testament had access to accurate information about what might happen 2000 years or more after they wrote, or that their vision of some final vindication and judgement is anything other than simply an impressive vision. It is a way of embodying hope, but agnosticism about the long-term future is probably the only sensible option.

Belief in an individual afterlife

More immediate for many people is the question of what, if anything, we can look forward to after our own death. Yet again it can only be a matter of speculation; none of us can know for certain. But what are the options open to us?

In 1995, Professor Douglas Davies, a Professor in the Theology Department of Durham University, worked with Alistair Shaw on the book *Reusing Old Graves*.[1] The purpose was to discover attitudes towards death that might have some bearing on the question of whether old grave spaces might be reused after a period. They carried out a significant sociological survey, inviting respondents to choose between five broad categories for what they believed about afterlife. Just over a third (34.1%) believed that 'the soul passes on'. Just under a third (28.8%) believed that life ends with death. Slightly fewer (21.7%) believed that it was 'in God's hands', substantially fewer (12.2%) believed in reincarnation, and even fewer (7.9%) believed in resurrection. Some held more than one belief.

Davies and Shaw broke down the responses according to those who had a religious affiliation and those who had none. Perhaps not surprisingly over two-thirds of atheists (68.8%) and just under two-thirds of agnostics (63%) believed death was the end of life, but the next largest group for atheists (17.4%) believed 'the soul passes on', while only five per cent of agnostics believed that. Perhaps it was also not surprising, given how relatively little is said in the Old Testament about any afterlife, to find that over half of the Jews surveyed (55%) believed death was the end of life, although a significant group (22.2%) believed in reincarnation.

---

1 Douglas Davies and Alistair Shaw (1995) *Reusing Old Graves.* Crayford: Shaw and Son.

Of those with affiliations to Christian churches, Davies and Shaw discovered that Anglicans were remarkably similar to the overall population. About a third (32%) believed death was the end of life, another third (33%) believed 'the soul passes on', but only a very small group (4%) believed in resurrection – an even smaller group than those (14%) who believed in reincarnation. Roman Catholics were different. Only a small group (14%) believed death was the end of life, a significantly larger number than Anglicans (18%) believed in resurrection, and nearly half (48%) believed 'the soul passes on'. A significant number of those with a religious affiliation (17% of Anglicans, 32 % of Roman Catholics) were prepared simply to say they 'trusted in God'.

In the 20 years that have elapsed since that survey, there are no clear statistics on what is believed today as far as I can discover, but it seems unlikely to be substantially very different. Of course, truth, as opposed to what people believe, cannot be identified by sociological statistics. But it is worth considering the options identified in that survey and perhaps to work out the criteria that might apply to making a decision between them.

Anglicans have always asserted that there are three sources of authority for Christian teaching: Scripture, Tradition and Reason, although some have also added a fourth of Experience. The difficulty in the case of any belief about an afterlife is that each of the first three might lead to different conclusions, while 'near-death experiences' can be interpreted in a variety of ways, none of which is reliable.

Some of those who say Scripture is the final authority conclude that a story about Jesus resolves the issue. At the time of Jesus, one Jewish group, the Sadducees, did not believe in any afterlife or resurrection. They were a priestly and aristocratic Jewish party from whom the High Priest was chosen, and they took their stand on the written law in the Pentateuch or first five books of the Old Testament, in which there is little evidence of any belief in a significant afterlife other than a rather shadowy existence in the place of the departed, Sheol. The Sadducees' denial of any resurrection was therefore traditionalist in character.

However, belief in life beyond death varied over the whole period the Old Testament was being written, and in the later period significant belief in the afterlife developed. Some of the books of the Apocrypha show the influence of Platonic thought about the immortality of the soul following the Hellenisation of much of the Mediterranean world by Alexander the Great. The Pharisees, who were a more populist Jewish movement, often opposed to the Sadducees, followed the oral law as well as the written law, and from that they found reasons for believing in individual judgement after death, eternal life, angels and spirits.

In Mark's Gospel there is an account, (Mark 12.18–27) repeated in both Matthew's and Luke's Gospels, of a question asked of Jesus by the Sadducees about the resurrection. The context was a question about seven brothers who had followed the advice of Deuteronomy 25 and married the living wife of one of the brothers after he and each of his subsequent brothers died. The Sadducees asked who would be the husband in heaven. Jesus' reply argued that there is no marriage in heaven and that the dead would be 'like angels'. The subsequent argument in the Gospel passage, which may have been used by Jesus or may have been a later addition taken from a Pharisaic answer, is based on the story of God speaking to Moses from the burning bush in Exodus 3.6 and saying, 'I am the God of Abraham, The God of Isaac, and the God of Jacob'. Jesus is reported as saying that God was the God of the living and not the dead, implying that Abraham, Isaac and Jacob must have survived death. To the modern mind that may not seem a conclusive argument, but it is clear that Jesus followed the Pharisees rather than the Sadducees on the matter of any afterlife.

That resolves the issue for some Christians, but it does not for all. The human Jesus was, after all, a product of the society of which he was a part, and arguments about any afterlife then were rooted in very different considerations from those that might apply today. It will not seem to every member of today's Church, to say nothing of those on the fringe or outside the Church, that they should conclude that just because Jesus said something it must be true now, in very different intellectual and cultural circumstances.

But what about Tradition? It is certainly the case that the tradition of the Church has generally taught that there is an afterlife, but in practice debates within the Church about any afterlife have often been consequent on what might be described as 'pastoral' issues. For example, one of the more difficult ecclesiastical debates has been about any belief in purgatory. Can there be any preparation for eternity? The appropriateness or otherwise of prayers for the dead has also been a ground for major controversy. If there is any afterlife, then many Christians would hold that purgatory, as some sort of preparation for being in the presence of God, would seem essential – not so much a place of punishment as a place for cleansing. Similarly, praying for the dead would seem a wholly pastoral activity for those who have suffered some major bereavement. That is now widely, though not universally, accepted and features as at least optional in funeral liturgies.

But those are less fundamental questions than the major one of whether it is possible to believe in any afterlife at all. That depends on what we think human beings really are. The

Church's tradition maintains that each person has a body, a spirit, and a soul. The body and even the mind might die, but the soul would somehow continue in some mysterious way, either in some 'other world' or, as it seems some still believe, in a form of reincarnation as another human being.

Reason might lead to other conclusions in today's world. It is very difficult to sustain the notion of a soul if our consciousness is wholly dependent on our physical brains. If, as many now hold, human beings are a psychosomatic unity where body and mind are held together, then when our brains cease to work, our consciousness must cease as well. As the brain surgeon Henry Marsh said, 'Neuroscience tells us that it is highly improbable that we have souls.'[2] I suspect, though cannot prove, that this is what lies behind the view of the significant proportion of churchgoers who simply say 'death is the end of life'.

In my experience, this is a matter rarely openly addressed in church circles, partly no doubt because in many cases it only emerges where someone has faced a recent bereavement, and there is an understandable reluctance to risk emotional distress. In such circumstances it is more often passed over in embarrassed silence, probably because many would also say that surely we cannot *know*. But when each of my parents died and I received letters from people telling me that they were living on in some other world, my own reaction was 'How do you know?' That was the start of a process that led me to my current conclusions. Although ultimate ignorance on the matter is inevitable, we can speculate, and, personally, I find the notion of any immortality of the individual soul at the very least unlikely for the reasons that Marsh gives.

2 Henry Marsh (2014) *Do No Harm: Stories of Life, Death and Brain Surgery.* London: Weidenfeld and Nicholson, p.200.

But what of the other possibility that Davies and Shaw identified? There are certainly those who assert that strictly orthodox Christian belief does not embrace immortality of the soul, but future resurrection. The model would be that of the Risen Jesus as the first fruits of a new creation, and the hope that such a resurrection awaits all those who believe. If that really is the case, it is remarkable that only four per cent of Anglicans believe it. I imagine again the problem is that many today find it very difficult to conceive of any lasting being that does not have some sort of material dimension. An ethereal 'spiritual' entity is very difficult to conceive given what we know about the relationship of the brain and the mind, while some sort of semi-physical resurrection seems highly unlikely. Where would the physical bit come from? Of course, resurrection can never be finally disproved, but I have to confess that personally I am not in the four per cent that believe it.

John Hick in his book *The New Frontier of Religion and Science*, which I mentioned in Chapter 3, has a chapter entitled 'After Death'. Because of his interest in, and creative engagement with, those of other faiths, he discusses the notion of reincarnation. He points out that in both Hindu and Buddhist philosophy:

> Conscious memories are not required by the understanding of re-incarnation…it is not the present conscious personality that is reborn, but a deeper element within us, our essential moral/spiritual nature, a basic dispositional structure which both affects and is affected by all that we do and undergo in the course of our lives.[3]

---

3 John Hick (2010) *The New Frontier of Religion and Science.* Basingstoke: Palgrave Macmillan, p.195.

But if I have no memory of that, and if that 'basic dispositional structure' is located somehow in our minds and brains, which I think it must be, then personally I do not find that notion very convincing even though it is widely held in many Eastern religions.

As I am the sort of Christian where reason ultimately trumps both scripture and tradition I am therefore in those third of Anglicans who believe that death is the end of any personal consciousness for each of us. I find I am not alone among Christians, including clergy, in thinking that. I once hinted at that suspicion in a sermon in Westminster Abbey when I said I was not expecting anything beyond death. That, as far as I know, is the only occasion someone complained in writing about an address of mine to the Dean! It is, perhaps, interesting that the complainant was an American, as it seems belief in life after death is more common in America than in England. It may well be that many English people in the congregation objected, but if so they did not say so, at least not to me.

I do understand that such a non-belief is difficult for those who hope there might be some sort of ultimate justice beyond death. Many wish for somewhere where wrongs can be righted, evil overcome, and goodness restored where it has been destroyed. That is a completely understandable desire and one that to some extent I share. I also willingly acknowledge that non-belief in any afterlife is easier for someone who has had a reasonably comfortable life – as, at least so far, I have had. But apart from the fact that the righting of all wrongs seems unlikely in any personal sense, it might also be rather obsessively self-centred. The desire for justice is a wholly proper one, and I rather hope that many people work for that in practical ways during their lives as I said in the first part of this chapter. But any honest observer of the world as it is and has been will see that many people did not receive justice during their lives, and went to their deaths knowing that. Some no doubt did so with an enormous sense of being permanently wronged, but it is remarkable that others appear to have accepted death with a measure of equanimity. I salute them for their honesty and, in a sense, their generosity in not demanding or expecting revenge.

I also recognise that there are some who simply fear death as a final extinction, and cling to Christian Faith as something that provides hope for some sort of reward after death. To the extent that no one can know for certain what happens after we die of course they might be right. But I can only say that while I in no way look forward to the process of dying, I am not sure that I fear death itself. Once I have died, I will no longer exist in time. But no one can take away the fact that I did once live, and to that extent my life will have become part of all that has been, which might be described as eternity. I am encouraged to find that Baroness Mary Warnock, who describes herself as a member of the Church of England and a regular attender, believes the same thing.[4] Personally, I do not feel the need to want more than that.

However, there is one other element to what might happen after our deaths that it is profitable to explore, and that is the memory of people. Our memory of someone can be changed both for good and for bad – look what happened to the memory of Jimmy Savile after his death. But I hope when I die there might at least be some people, my family if no more, who might remember me at least for a period.

As I said in the discussion of consciousness in Chapter 3, the remarkable thing about human consciousness is that while our personal consciousness is always ultimately inaccessible to

---

4 Mary Warnock in Bel Mooney (ed.) (2003) *Devout Sceptics: Conversations on Faith and Doubt*. London: Hodder and Stoughton, pp.169–78.

anyone else, we are influenced by one another. In some cases, that influence can be long lasting and profound. This is where the nature of Jesus Christ after his death becomes significant. I realise that some Christians say that they have a personal relationship with the Risen Christ that is more than simply holding him and all that he was in their memory, but I have to wonder what that 'more' might really mean. I will discuss that in the later chapter on prayer and worship. But it is possible to have a very active memory of someone, and even begin to interrogate that memory in some way that can be creative. Active reflection on the memory of Christ can certainly make a difference to how people behave, and just possibly active reflection on the lives of others we have known but who have died might also make a difference. So I believe that memory might hold a clue for making some sort of sense of death, because the memory of us does live on. That is personally how I try to make sense of what is said about resurrection in, say, a funeral service.

The memory of me, and of far greater men and women than me, has a lasting and eternal element to it. If I remain, at least for a short period, in the memory of others, maybe it is not wholly impossible to imagine that others, and I, might also remain in the memory of God. Quite what that means I do not know, although I do not personally think it implies any continued personal consciousness. But for me it is enough.

For further reading

Douglas Davies and Alistair Shaw (1995) *Reusing Old Graves.* Crayford: Shaw and Sons.

C.H. Dodd (1936) *The Apostolic Teaching and its Developments*. London: Hodder and Stoughton.

Bel Mooney (ed.) (2003) *Devout Sceptics: Conversations about Faith and Doubt.* London: Hodder and Stoughton.

Vernon White (2006) *Life Beyond Death*. London: Darton, Longman and Todd.

9

PRAYER AND PUBLIC WORSHIP

The Christian Faith is not simply a subject for thinking; it also encourages encountering God through prayer and public worship. What might that entail?

Prayer

Prayer as a way of relating to God is fundamental, but what exactly are we praying for? If the notion of God that I put forward in Chapter 3 is correct, then it follows that it cannot be a way of trying to get God to do something that he would not otherwise do. Battering on the gates of heaven to ask God to change something may be the way some Christians view the matter, but it suffers from at least two problems. First, the notion of God intervening in the events of the world means that presumably he could also intervene in matters that are obviously dreadful, yet manifestly he does not do so, or does not do so effectively. For every example that some might give of prayers having been answered there are other examples where they were not. The experience of events like the Holocaust or tsunamis shows that. Secondly, human beings have free will. While someone might want to cooperate with God's purposes for the world, God does not seem to want to force people to act in that way. It is a sign of genuine love that it never tries to compel, and that may be true of God's love as well. The choice of how to act remains ours.

But that does not remove the possibility of prayer pointing to something significant and real. If, at the heart of everything, we experience not only the claims of pursuing truth, goodness and beauty, but also the possibility of love, albeit a love that is sometimes thwarted, then prayer can be a way of aligning our wills to that heart of everything. That is easier to understand in the first two traditional areas of prayer, thanksgiving and confession.

Except for those unfortunate enough to be in a totally dire situation, most people can think of things for which they are grateful. Acknowledging that, even if only in our own minds, is probably a good thing to do from time to time, and may help give us a balanced view of our situation, particularly if we are also aware of frustrations in our lives. Counting your blessings might sound pious, but it might also be sensible. Thanking God in that way does not mean that we consider every good thing we experience is a personal gift from him, but it is rather a recognition that the world is as it is, and for many people that includes a whole variety of encounters with what is good and fulfilling. If God is the reason why anything is there in the first place, it can be no bad thing from time to time to thank him for what is good. Being grateful can encourage a wider emotional generosity in return.

Similarly, acknowledging specific failures and more fundamental faults in our make-up is also a sensible path to self-awareness. Wallowing in a sense of being wicked probably does no one any good; I am not suggesting that we should adopt the Book of Common Prayer's phrase that we are all 'miserable offenders'. But in almost everyone there is a curious mixture of altruism and selfishness. None of us are perfect, and acknowledging that, even if only to ourselves, is healthy. Forgiveness, by God and of others, is part of the Lord's Prayer – 'forgive us our trespasses as we forgive those who trespass against us' – and that God forgives is a basic Christian understanding of his nature. I discuss the matter of forgiveness in greater depth in the next chapter.

The Church has also offered confession to a priest as a means of helping an individual deal with any feelings of personal guilt. The Anglican stance on whether to make a confession has been that 'all may, some should, no one must'. That has always seemed to me wise advice. Of course, if someone confesses a crime, then it is always open to a priest to withhold absolution until the person concerned has told the appropriate authorities. I have personally heard confessions occasionally, and most penitents have not committed crimes, although some might feel guilty about having been the victim of crime, but that is a complex area that lies beyond the scope of this book. My point here is that confession, whether to God alone or to a priest, is an important part of the Christian experience of prayer.

Relating what we feel grateful for and what we feel bad about in the context of our relationship with what is at the heart of everything, which I presume to call God, might therefore be a very natural thing for many people to do even if they do not use the word God. But what about asking for things we want?

Most of us can quite easily identify things that we want. If we pray for them, we are looking at our wishes, but then seeking to align them to what is at the heart of everything. In that process, our personal interrogating, the memory we have of Jesus as revealed in the Gospels can come into its own. In that context, some of what we want will be revealed as frankly self-centred. Praying for such things might show that and make us modify our wishes.

However, we might want some things for other people that are not purely selfish, healing for a sick person for example, or for peace in some sorts of conflicts. Is there any point in praying for matters like that? That depends on what we are praying for. If we are asking simply that God will wave some sort of magic wand and make something happen, then I doubt whether that will do much good. But our praying for it might also make us examine what we want. Is it realistic, and what, if anything, might we do to make that situation better? To pray is to risk being changed.

I can certainly think of examples of situations where I have felt driven to my knees. Visiting the site of Dachau concentration camp many years ago was one, where I was very grateful that a group of nuns had a chapel built on the edge of the site, where anyone could go to pray. The most obvious prayer then was that nothing like that should ever happen in the world again, but it was no good praying for that if it did not force me to think of what I could do to contribute to a world where that would not happen. Similar feelings were generated when, in Calcutta, I visited a *bustee* with the Cathedral Relief Service many years ago. Some polluted cooking oil had been sold that meant many of those there, in addition to the conditions of appalling poverty in which they lived, were also faced with the challenge of being blind, which, if they were lucky, might only be temporary. Praying for that situation would have been pointless unless it also made me contribute financially to those institutions that were trying to do something about it, and to reflect more widely on how such gross inequalities in the world could be lessened. In both of those cases, prayer was part of a process of making me change – and that might be how God works. Prayer is an activity that can make those who pray agents for change, as happened in South Africa towards the end of apartheid and in

East Germany just before the Berlin Wall came down. If prayer only made the person doing the praying change in some way, it would still be worthwhile.

But those being prayed for might also experience something. When I was ordained in St Paul's Cathedral many years ago, I have never forgotten the sense that there were a number of people praying for me, which I found encouraging. In many other areas of life as well, to surround someone with a sense of loving concern may well have a beneficial effect on them, as when a sick person knows that others are thinking of them. This is not to say that prayer is any form of magic solution, but if someone in need knows that others are genuinely concerned for them that sense might itself be part of a therapeutic process happening at a semi-conscious level. Many doctors would say that a patient's morale can have an effect on their healing.

And that might happen not simply to individuals. When the search for a peace process in Northern Ireland was going on, there was quite a lot of prayer offered for it in churches. Did the knowledge of that prayer have any effect on the individuals engaged? I do not know, but it would be foolish to dismiss the possibility that realising that many other people were placing their hopes on a process in which they were engaged might strengthen the determination to achieve something worthwhile. So while I do not have any magical view of prayer, I certainly believe it can be a worthwhile process in which to engage. Perhaps one can never know any more than that.

Public worship

I have been fortunate enough to attend many acts of public worship that were inspiring, but equally I have attended many that were not! There are many things that can go wrong, whether it is the music being poor, the words being banal or the address being implausible. Those responsible for conducting public worship have a significant responsibility.

However, joining together with others in some public act of worship has always been part of Christian discipleship, and it is both a personal and a corporate act. It is personal in the sense that any individual worshipper brings their own concerns and their own ways of thinking about God. With luck, the public act of worship will provide some elements that each individual can make their own. But it is also corporate in that the worshipper is not acting purely for themselves but with others. There are two dimensions to that.

First, at least in the case of a body like the Church of England, it will be an act in a parish church, which exists for everyone who lives in that parish. There will be a vicarious element in the worship; it is being done on behalf of the whole community. Many a worshipper, if passing an acquaintance on the way to church, might be asked 'Say one for me!' It might be a light-hearted statement, but it should not be dismissed just for that. Many who may not pray much themselves like to know that others are praying for them. Worship is done for the whole community.

Secondly, it is being done as part of a Christian community that stretches not only over a place, but also over time. That is most obvious in the words that are used. The Nicene Creed for example, used in the service of Holy Communion, was first formulated in the fourth century, when Constantine, the first Roman Emperor to become a Christian, tried to unite the various forms of Christian belief present in his empire. There was a conflict within the Church about how to view the person of Christ, and the Nicene Creed was an attempt, partially successful, to find a form of words that would hold the churches together. The thought forms of the fourth century were very different from those that would be natural today, but the Church still uses those words, not because they are necessarily the best way of describing what Christians believe today, but because they did express how the Church at one point explained its faith. The contemporary believer might want to identify with the body that once put it like that.

In the Book of Common Prayer the Creed starts with 'I believe', which is what the Bishops at the Council of Nicaea were asked to sign. More recently the Church of England has instead started the creed with 'We believe', reflecting the fact that this is a corporate belief that was once expressed like that. There is more on this matter in Chapter 11, but the point is that the words used in services, not just in the creeds, but in hymns and prayers as well, come from over a very long period of Christian history. The individual in Church might well find themselves saying or singing things that, left to themselves, they may not put quite like that, but it is in the nature of a corporate body that individual interpretations are caught up in institutional formularies. Personally, I have rarely found that much of a problem, although I am certainly aware of others who find times when, metaphorically at least, they need to cross their fingers behind their backs in some hymns. I can only sing the first verse of the hymn 'Jerusalem' by reflecting that if the words are taken literally the answer to every question is 'No'!

Corporate worship is more than words. The service of Holy Communion, which has been at least a weekly part of my life for many years, has at its heart four symbolic actions, when Jesus took the bread and wine, blessed them, broke the bread, and gave it to his disciples. Except in John's Gospel, all those elements are present in the four accounts of the event in the New Testament (Matthew 26.26–9; Mark 14.22–5;

Luke 22.15–20; 1 Corinthians 11.23–5), although their order varies and the exact words used are not identical. But it does seem highly likely that Jesus had a final supper with his disciples shortly before he died and that is the basis of the service of Holy Communion. In the 2000 years that have happened since the first event, those symbolic actions have been interpreted in all sorts of ways, and meanings have been found that go beyond what might have been intended in the first meal, but that sort of elaboration of meaning is what naturally happens to a symbolic act. Personally, I find the way Bishop John Robinson brought out their significance in his book *Liturgy Coming to Life* still resonates.[1]

Consider the first action, when Jesus took the bread. In many churches now that takes the form of an offertory procession, where members of the congregation present the bread and wine to the priest taking the service. But who pays for the bread and wine? The costs of that in the context of the whole running of a church are not great, but symbolically they are very important. In the Church of England it is the churchwardens, the representatives of the laity, who are responsible for producing the elements, and they use the collections provided by the congregation. The bread and the wine can therefore be seen as the gifts of the people, produced by the money they have given. It is not fanciful to reflect on how that money was earned and to see all human life, some good some bad, reflected in the elements that are being presented. Yet, in the Eucharist, that is what is taken and then given back to the people as the body and blood of Christ.

The priest then blesses the elements. Wars were fought over the meaning of that at the time of the Reformation; was this

1 John A.T. Robinson (1960) *Liturgy Coming to Life.* London: Mowbray and Co.

simply a memorial meal or were the bread and wine changed in some way through that act of blessing? One way of looking at it now is to see that the process of blessing is simply to bring something back into a right relationship with the God who ultimately is behind all that is. The act of blessing recognises the way God is there in everything, but is now seen as being especially present in those elements. The bread and wine are still bread and wine, but they convey so much more when seen in that symbolic context.

Then comes the great climax of the action, the breaking of the bread. 'This is my body, which is given for you. Do this in remembrance of me.' Christ's body was broken on the cross, and that sacrificial act is remembered and re-enacted in the Eucharist. The sacrificial action of Jesus at his crucifixion is seen as the event at the very heart of any Christian community and that is what gives it is cohesion and life.

That is what is then given to the congregation. People in all sorts of varied conditions might be present in a service, but they are all invited to share the bread and wine. At the communion rail there are no favourites. All are united in the one act of eating and drinking the symbolic sacrifice of Christ and literally taking that life into themselves. That can break down all social and other divisions, for at the altar the people are united, not by being good, or being grand, or being important in whatever role they have in life, but simply by receiving the sacrificial life of Christ and finding a unity that transcends, or should transcend, all divisions. At the foot of the Cross all need forgiveness and acceptance, and that is what is offered. We meet and share as penitent sinners.

That way of looking at the Eucharist has been important to me for over 50 years, and although I have all sorts of questions about many aspects of the Christian Faith, that remains at the core of worship. It is the same whether it is a quiet said service with a few people, or a grand event with wonderful music in a packed church. God comes to us in the form of bread and wine.

I know I am not alone in combining a certain questioning stance about Christian theology with a more traditional and dignified approach to worship. Lots of things can, and sometimes do spoil worship, an inept sermon for example, or some ludicrous prejudice revealing itself in the congregation. But most of the time worship does its role for me, expresses the fact that I am part of a corporate community, and that provides sustenance for the soul. That is why I go week by week.

For further reading

Peter Baelz (1982) *Does God Answer Prayer?* London: Darton, Longman and Todd.

John A. T. Robinson (1960) *Liturgy Coming to Life.* London: Mowbray and Co.

10

LIVING AS A CHRISTIAN

Some Contemporary Issues

According to Matthew, Mark and Luke Jesus gave two commandments to his followers; 'to love God with all your heart, with all your soul and with all your mind' and 'to love your neighbour as yourself' (Matthew 22.37–8; Mark 12.30–1; Luke 10.27). I have tried so far in this book to say what might be entailed by the first commandment, perhaps particularly by the phrase to love God 'with all your mind', but what of loving your neighbour as yourself? Christianity at its best is as much concerned with right action as with right belief. What are the distinctively Christian aspects of loving your neighbour as yourself?

There are huge areas of national and international life where that is a testing notion. Perhaps the area of war and peace is one of the most complex. Winston Churchill is reported to have said in a White House lunch that 'to jaw-jaw is always better than to war-war'. That must be so, and if war must come it should only ever be as a last resort. But sometimes the evil that is being done to others makes such an extreme action necessary. Hitler's treatment of the Jews would be one example, and possibly Daish's treatment of its prisoners is another. I am not a pacifist, but war is always a defeat of diplomacy.

A second huge area is that the disparities in wealth in our world and even within our nation is a challenge that 'loving our neighbour' must reflect upon. In terms of the life of our nation it must be disturbing to anyone with a conscience that the disparities in income are as great as they are. That some chief executives in the UK earn over 800 times the average income of their employees even a former Conservative MP describes as 'troubling'.[1] Only government action could make much effect on that, but there seems little desire for such action at the moment. On the international scale the disparities are even greater. According to Oxfam, 62 people in the world own as much as the poorer half of the world's population. Thankfully some of those individuals are very generous in their charitable giving, but the inequalities are alarming. There are no simple solutions, as I discovered years ago in Bangladesh. I can only note that a deep and sacrificial care for the poor is not just an option for any serious Christian. It represents a core value.

However, it is not my intention in this chapter to provide some sort of wide-ranging review of Christian moral philosophy, if for no other reason because I probably do not have the knowledge or ability to do it. But I am aware that 'loving your neighbour' is not just a theoretical way of responding to other people; it has to be translated into practical action in specific areas. There are many matters where what it might mean to love your neighbour as yourself is both difficult yet critical, and I have chosen four to consider, each of which has a contemporary resonance, and on the last two of which I find myself in some disagreement with official episcopal statements. Being sceptical

1 *The Times* 22.1.16 'Wealth gap shows that capitalism is failing' by Matthew Parris.

does not only apply to belief, it might even apply to some moral judgements.

Forgiveness

Jesus demonstrated the centrality of forgiveness in the parable of the Prodigal Son (Luke 15.11–32), when the son decided to ask for forgiveness from his the father, but the father offered it before the son even had the chance to say so. It was a central part of the Lord's Prayer: 'Forgive us our trespasses as we forgive those who trespass against us' (Matthew 6.2; Luke 11.4), with the implication that his followers both received God's forgiveness and should offer it to others. In Matthew's Gospel Peter asked Jesus how often he should forgive his brother, 'as many as seven times?' and Jesus replied 'I do not say to you seven times, but seventy times seven' (Matthew 18.21–2; Matthew 18.23–35). There then follows the parable of the servant who was let off a huge debt by a king, but the servant then demanded far smaller debts be repaid from those who owed him. The king responded by having the servant thrown into prison, and the parable ends: 'So also my heavenly Father will do to every one of you, if you do not forgive your brother from your heart.' Perhaps most fundamentally, according to Luke, Jesus demonstrated it by forgiving those who crucified him: 'Father forgive them; for they do not know what they do'(Luke 23.34). Whether that was actually said by the historical Jesus at the time of the crucifixion is problematical; the other Gospel writers do not mention it, but it certainly seems wholly consistent with the teaching that Jesus gave during his lifetime about forgiveness. Forgiveness, by God and of others, was central to his teaching, even to the extent of Jesus being reported as saying that we should love our enemies (Matthew 5.43; Luke 6.27).

What does that mean in practice today? In Chapter 6, I discussed the notion of being forgiven, or as Paul Tillich put it, being accepted by God. But what of us forgiving others?

I am fortunate in being someone who has not really received at the hands of others any real harm. I have certainly been irritated by others, enough to know that even forgiving their words or deeds can be quite difficult, and I have experienced enough to know that often fault is not just on one side. A disagreement over even something quite minor can flare into a dispute where each side responds to one attack by another. I also know of those who would say of such situations 'Do not get angry, get even!' Yet that sort of mutual tit-for-tat recrimination can so easily lead to destructive conflicts that will adversely affect both parties. A simple act of forgiving can break the spell and lead to a more healthy way of living. This is not an exclusively Christian notion; no one has put it better than Jonathan Sacks, the former Chief Rabbi. According to him, forgiveness is:

> more than a technique for conflict resolution. It is a stunningly original strategy. In a world without forgiveness evil begets evil, harm generates harm, and there is no way short of exhaustion or forgetfulness of breaking the sequence. Forgiveness breaks the chain. It introduces into the logic of interpersonal encounter the unpredictability of grace. It represents a decision not to do what instinct and passion urge us to do. It answers hate with a refusal to hate, animosity with generosity. Few more daring ideas have ever entered the human situation. Forgiveness means that we are not destined endlessly to replay the grievances of yesterday. It is the ability to live with the past without being held captive by the past. It would not be an exaggeration to say that forgiveness is the most compelling testimony to human freedom. It is about the action that is not reaction. It is the refusal to be defined by circumstance. It represents our ability to change course,

> reframe the narrative of the past and create an unexpected set of possibilities for the future.[2]

But while that might be possible in some acts of harm that human beings do to one another, what about the situations of much greater harm? The example shown by Gordon Wilson is worth reflecting on. His daughter was killed and he was injured in the IRA bombing at Enniskillen on Remembrance Sunday in 1987. Very shortly after the bombing he said on the BBC that he forgave the bombers, and asked for no retaliation from loyalist forces. His stance was very influential within Northern Ireland and made a significant contribution towards the peace process, although it also occasioned a good deal of criticism from those who saw showing forgiveness without repentance on the part of those who carried out the atrocity as excusing their behaviour. Wilson himself distinguished between showing forgiveness and excusing, and he never asked that the bombers should not be brought to justice. But he believed that, as a Christian, seeking reconciliation and peace even after an event like that was more important than continuing the conflict. Wilson himself continued that work of reconciliation, met those who had planned the bombing and pleaded with them, unsuccessfully, to give up their bombing campaign. The Irish Prime Minister made him a member of the Irish Senate. He died in 1995.

That does seem to me to be a fine example of the sort of forgiveness of which Jesus spoke. It is not ignoring the proper demands of justice, but it is offering forgiveness as a way of building relationships that might eventually lead to reconciliation. For the reconciliation to be effective, repentance on the part of the bombers would no doubt have been necessary,

---

2 Jonathan Sacks (2003) *The Dignity of Difference*. London: Continuum, p. 178 f.

but it was not a condition of offering forgiveness in the first place.

But that was Wilson forgiving those who had done great personal harm to him and to a member of his family. What about forgiving those who have caused great harm to others?

Simon Wiesenthal (1908–2005) was a Jewish prisoner of the Nazis and spent the period after the war tracking down those who had committed atrocities during the Holocaust. In his book *The Sunflower* he recounts an event while he was a prisoner during the war working in a hospital. He was asked to see a dying SS Officer, who wanted to confess to a Jew the terrible things he had been involved in against other Jews, and asked for Wiesenthal, as a representative Jew, to forgive him. Wiesenthal could not, and walked away in silence, although he continued to wonder whether he was right to do so.[3]

In those circumstances, I can fully understand and sympathise with his reaction. But a Christian priest in such circumstances is in a different position. As a human being he would no doubt feel as strongly as Wiesenthal did about the evil nature of the atrocities committed, but a priest also stands as a representative of the Christian Church, whose very existence is based on being a community of those who have known the forgiveness of God. The priest is certainly not free to ignore the legal demands of justice, and may, as I explained in the previous chapter, withhold absolution until a person who has committed a crime has made a proper public confession to the police. But that was not possible in the hospital; the law in Germany at the time did not recognise what was done to Jews in the Holocaust as crimes, and in any case the German soldier was dying. The soldier clearly understood the nature of what he had done as he

3 Simon Wiesenthal (1998) *The Sunflower: On the Possibilities and Limits of Forgiveness.* New York: Schocken.

was, in effect, making a deathbed confession. A priest would no doubt have made sure that he fully understood the evil that had been done and the need for total repentance, but a priest could then assure the soldier not of the forgiveness of the Jewish people, which was not in his gift, but of God's forgiveness, and so to enable the soldier at the point of death to be reconciled to God.

These are, of course, extreme situations, and fortunately very few people will ever find themselves in such positions, but it is often only in extreme situations that the underlying principles become clear. Forgiveness can come from below, as a human reaction to healing a relationship, but it can also come in response to above, from recognition that God's forgiveness of others should provoke a forgiving spirit towards others, as the Lord's Prayer suggests. No one can suggest it is easy, particularly when the crime is as heinous as those done to Jewish people in the Holocaust, but forgiveness is not an option for Christian living; it is at its very core.

Interfaith engagement

In the United Kingdom our neighbour often includes those of other faiths from our own. One friend of mine believes that the apparently conflicting relations between different religions is further ground for scepticism by some people, with them almost wanting to say 'a plague on all your houses'! But in fact some very good work in encouraging healthy and honest relations between different faiths has happened over a number of years.

The London Society of Jews and Christians was founded in 1927, and during the Second World War the national 'Council for Christians and Jews' (CCJ) was established. When I was at Westminster Abbey, I became the chairman of the

Central London branch of CCJ, and one of our early events in the Abbey involved a joint Hannukah/Advent Service, when the candles for the Jewish Hannukah service were lit, as were the Christian Advent Candles. It was a very moving event that brought a large congregation of both Jews and Christians to the Abbey. Later I was involved in bringing a young Palestinian and a young Israeli to talk at one of our meetings about their lives and their commitment to One Voice, an organisation that seeks in Israel and Palestine to bring together representatives from both communities in working for a two-states solution to the conflict. As a result of that I was invited by the British branch of One Voice to speak at a meeting of university students from various universities across England about Christian attitudes to the Holy Land, and there were also there a Jewish rabbi talking about Jewish attitudes and a Moslem Imam talking about Moslem attitudes.

The three of us got on so well that we agreed we should continue to work together on these matters. One of the ways the three faiths link together is through 'Scriptural Reasoning', where readings from the Old Testament, the Koran and the New Testament on a common theme are considered together. We decided to hold in Westminster Abbey's Jerusalem Chamber a Scriptural Reasoning session on the subject of Jerusalem and involved a mixed group from all three faiths looking together at the passages.

This was so successful that we then decided to take some of those involved to Northern Ireland to see for ourselves how the peace process was working and whether it had implications for the conflict in the Middle East. For many years, the Republicans in Northern Ireland have had a great sympathy for the Palestinian cause and the Loyalists for Israel, so the parallels are recognised locally. The peace process is itself a great achievement, but it still has not produced a community wholly at ease with itself, and we saw examples of both the positive achievements and some of the more negative forces still at work there. It was a very worthwhile thing to do, perhaps illustrated by the remark of one of the rabbis present who said at the end 'this has made me realise we must talk to our enemies'.

Such interfaith discussions enable those of different faiths to discover what is obvious, that whatever faith we might belong to we share a common humanity. Friendships formed across religious divides are not only humanly valuable but symbolically so as well. Sadly, though, in all faiths there are some whose loyalty to their own faith results in a sort of tribalism, when they are more concerned with defending the truth they see in their own religion than engaging openly with those of different perspectives.

A helpful perspective on that was provided by a conference on relations between world religions organised by the Theology Department of Birmingham University in 1970. The Professor of Theology at Birmingham at the time, John Hick, wrote in the subsequent report:

> Instead of asking, 'Which religion is true – Christianity, or Hinduism, or Islam…?' we can see these religions as historic streams of human life, each of which may be built partly upon truth and partly upon error. Instead then of asking whether a religion, as such, is true in some absolute sense we are free to recognise religious truth, wherever it is evident, within all man's cultures and civilisations.[4]

He quotes Wilfred Cantrell Smith in *Questions of Religious Truth*:

---

4 John Hick (1974) *Truth and Dialogue: The Relationship Between World Religions.* London: Sheldon Press, p.142.

> Christianity, I would suggest, is not absolutely true, impersonally, statistically; rather it can *become* true, if as you and I appropriate it to ourselves and interiorise it, insofar as we live it out from day to day. It becomes true as we take it off the shelf and personalise it, in dynamic actual existence.[5]

Hick points out that there are still truth claims to be tested in any religion, and simply to say that a faith is lived and believed by an individual does not of itself make it true. 'The life is not good if the "knowledge" on which it is based is not knowledge at all but delusion.'[6] It is on the basis of that argument that I personally would like to see those of no religion included in interfaith discussions; they might well have a helpful perspective to bring to bear.

Later Hick wrote:

> It is possible to consider the hypothesis that the great religions are all, at their experiential roots, in contact with the same divine reality, but that their differing experiences of that reality, intersecting over the centuries with the different thought forms of different cultures, have led to considerable elaboration... However, now that, in the 'one world' of today, the religious traditions are consciously interesting with each other in mutual observation and inter-faith dialogue, it is possible that their future developments may be on gradually converging courses.[7]

Whether he will be proved correct about convergence obviously remains to be seen. It requires individual believers to be free of tribalism and open to others, and sadly all religions have groups who are neither. But interfaith dialogue is alive and well in many parts of the world today, and sometimes the biggest

5 Hick, *Truth and Dialogue*, p.143.

6 Hick, *Truth and Dialogue*, p.148.

7 Hick, *Truth and Dialogue*, p.151.

conflicts are within religions rather than between them. A serious commitment to 'love your neighbour as yourself' is a good starting place for such engagement.

Assisting those facing death

Like any priest, I have, from time to time, ministered to those who were dying. It is never easy and is sometimes emotionally draining, but on most occasions it is reasonably straightforward. Fears and anxieties can be talked about honestly; prayers can be said if that is what the patient wishes, and the end of life approached with dignity and compassion. But there are a few cases where difficult questions about the appropriate medical and spiritual care arise, and some involve very complicated moral dilemmas, which is why I have included this section in this chapter.

We are each influenced by our own experiences, and I must recount one that happened to me many years ago. I well remember going with my mother when I was much younger to visit an elderly aunt who was over 80 years old. She had asked us to visit her, because she was sure she was dying. We saw her in hospital, and although she was seriously ill, she still had a clear mind and said she had had a good life and was 'ready to go'. We then watched with some horror as a doctor administered a large dose of antibiotics. When my mother asked whether that was wise, the doctor treated her as simply a greedy relative wanting her aunt's possessions, which was very far from the truth; my mother's concern was simply that her aunt's wishes should be respected. The result of the injection and further treatment was that my aunt had another six months of frustrating misery in hospital until she finally died. I wrote to the doctor afterwards saying what had happened, but received no reply.

It made me realise that doctors are far from infallible in treating those who are dying. They will, of course, plead the Hippocratic Oath, which is sometimes mistranslated to include the phrase 'I will do no harm.' But it seemed to my mother and to me that actively taking steps to continue my aunt's life when she was content and ready to die was itself 'doing harm'. That certainly influenced me when, many years later, my mother herself was dying in hospital. I asked the doctors to keep her without pain but not to seek to revive her, as I knew for certain that was what she wanted. Fortunately the medical staff then respected my request.

Medial science has now got to a level where it is often possible to keep people alive when they might otherwise die. But death will come to all of us eventually, and simply prolonging life even when it will be miserable does not to my mind serve any good purpose. Allowing people to die rather than intervening to keep them alive for what will almost certainly be a miserable future may sometimes be the best course. As far as possible that choice should be made by the individual patient when they are in their right mind, and when the medical evidence is clear that there is very little chance of any significant recovery. I have therefore written to my doctor to say that should I ever be taken seriously ill, in such circumstances I do not want medical staff simply to prevent my death. I have given copies of that letter to my wife and daughter in the hope that if I am taken ill and treated by emergency medical staff, my family will have time to pass on that request. Many other people I know feel the same. Of course, if a person feels otherwise and would prefer to be kept alive for as long as possible, that choice should certainly also be available and respected, but I am not convinced it should be automatically imposed.

The difficulty facing doctors is that many people do not make their wishes known and it is left to them, sometimes in conversation with grieving and possibly distraught next-of-kin, to decide what to do. I, and I am sure many others, have great sympathy for doctors in such circumstances having to consider what constitutes 'Do no harm.'

But what of the more complicated matter of assisted dying? If someone is close to death should medical staff be free to help him or her die? It is not as though such things have never happened in the past. It has emerged that when King George V was dying of cancer, was already unconscious and had only a few hours to live, his physician, Lord Dawson, administered a mixture of morphine and cocaine knowing that he would then die before midnight. Dawson considered this preserved the King's dignity and helped the Royal Family through what might otherwise have been a very difficult period. What caused more consternation when it finally emerged was that he also thought this would enable the King's death to be reported in the morning newspapers rather than the more sensational evening papers of the time. This only became public when Dawson's diaries were discovered many years after his own death. Whether he consulted the close relatives of the King is not known, but there can be no doubt that the physician considered his own motives honourable, even if now some question his decision. Dawson spoke later in a House of Lords debate against euthanasia, but on the grounds he believed such decisions did not belong to the law but should be the preserve of medical staff alone. Today, similar matters are very closely watched in any medical context and any doctor acting to help someone die knows that they are liable to be reported and even prosecuted, so inevitably the matter now comes to the law and to parliament.

There are many cases that probably happen every day in hospitals where doctors administer drugs such as morphine for the sake of pain relief, while recognising that a side effect of such drugs may be to shorten life. Very few would quibble at such decisions and doctors can quite properly plead that the medicine was designed primarily for pain relief. But there are those who want the law to go further to allow doctors to administer drugs with the specific intention of bringing forward death in the case of those who asked for that. At the moment, the law says that while suicide itself is not illegal, assisting someone to commit suicide is, so any doctor involved in that faces prosecution.

One of the major problems of any legislation that might change that is the effect it might have on vulnerable people being pressurised to agree to something that in fact they may not want. It is this desire to protect the vulnerable that has led many, including the Bishops of the Church of England, to oppose any change in the law. I totally recognise the need for extreme caution in this area and am certainly opposed to any general law permitting widespread euthanasia. But after some very high profile cases of individuals seeking the right to receive medical assistance to die, in 2010 the Director of Public Prosecutions (DDP), recognising that his department had to take decisions on whether to bring specific cases to court, issued public guidelines on the factors that might lead towards his staff deciding to bring a case and those which might discourage them from doing so. At the time many, including me, thought that was a very helpful clarification, and indeed I preached on that matter in the Abbey in support of the DPP's action.

Much of what the DPP said was clearly wise, for example that factors that would lead against bringing a prosecution would be that:

> the victim had reached a voluntary, clear, settled and informed decision to commit suicide; the suspect was wholly motivated by compassion; the suspect had sought to dissuade the victim from taking the course of action which resulted in his or her suicide; the actions of the suspect may be characterised as reluctant encouragement or assistance in the face of a determined wish on the part of the victim to commit suicide.

What though, on further reflection, is more difficult is that one of the factors in the guidelines making prosecution more likely is that:

> the suspect was acting in his or her capacity as a medical doctor, nurse, other healthcare professional, a professional carer (whether for payment or not), or as a person in authority, such as a prison officer, and the victim was in his or her care.

The intention behind that was clearly to ensure that the any patient could be confident the relationship with the doctor and carers could not be used to kill them off. But if a victim has made an informed decision to commit suicide, then it is surely better that they should do so with the help of qualified medical staff; a botched attempt at suicide in such cases would be the worst of all outcomes. What the guidelines allow is that relatives motivated wholly by compassion may assist the patient to go to the Dignitas clinic in Switzerland, where euthanasia is allowed under Swiss law, but not all families are able to afford this. It could also be claimed that the guidelines suggest action would not be taken against any doctor who assisted in the suicide of someone who was not in their care, but it is quite difficult to conceive the circumstances where that might be possible for many who might want such assistance.

I was invited some time ago to join a group of clergy, the chairman of whom is a rabbi, to think further about the issue.

We meet on a regular basis and recently heard from a specialist in palliative care who told us there are certain medical conditions where palliative care is not effective. The Bill sponsored by Lord Falconer that was before Parliament during 2014–15 and debated by the House of Commons in September 2015 was designed to deal with such cases. It limited itself to medical cases where doctors thought that a patient had less than six months to live, and where the patient had made it clear that they freely wanted medical assistance to die. An important change made during its passage through Parliament was an amendment passed by the House of Lords that said that each case should be reviewed by the Family Division of the High Court and that the Court should ensure that the conditions of the Bill were met, including the critical one that this this was a genuinely free decision by the patient and not one forced on them by others.

In the final debate in the House of Commons, where each member was allowed to follow their own conscience on a free vote, the Bill was rejected by 330 votes to 118. The Hansard report of the debate shows that the factors that led many to oppose the Bill were varied. There was for some a completely understandable reluctance to cross the present legal barrier preventing anyone assisting in someone else's death, and certainly such a grave decision would be a big change in the law. Some saw this as the thin edge of a wedge and that thereafter there would be pressure to make euthanasia more available, although any further change would still require the approval of Parliament. There were also those who thought the guidelines issued by the Director of Public Prosecutions in 2010 were sufficient and should be allowed a further test to time. Some also questioned the 'six months to live' element in the Bill, partly because some thought such a detailed prognosis was very difficult for doctors to be sure about, while others thought in some particularly hard cases it was very unlikely that people would die naturally in six months, although the patients concerned clearly wanted to die.

Parliament's decision, and particularly the size of the majority against in the House of Commons, means that it is unlikely to be brought before Parliament again in the near future. But it also seems probable the issue will not go away. The medical profession is clearly divided amongst itself. Although the vast majority of Church of England bishops are against any change in the law, one current Bishop has spoken in favour of it and there are a number of clergy, including George Carey, the former Archbishop of Canterbury, who feel that the claims of compassion for those enduring intolerable suffering mean they would support a change in the law. If opinion polls are to be believed (and some certainly question whether the main one on this subject is objective) the majority of the population think the law should be changed. The contention is that as suicide is legal in the United Kingdom, the fact that someone is not physically able to take that action should not prevent it happening if they genuinely so wished.

For that reason, as I have told the rabbi who chairs our group, I am on that side – but only just. It is one of the great moral dilemmas of our time and I doubt it is ever going to be easily resolved. Loving your neighbour often involves such very difficult questions.

Human sexuality

My final matter is, I suspect, one most people in this country have no real difficulty about. But the question of sexual orientation has been a divisive issue within the churches, and it continues to dominate much of the press discussions about the Church of England, so I have included it here.

For many years, I tried to avoid preaching on the subject of sex, because much of what was said in the Church seemed hypocritical and dishonest, and I had no desire to risk adding to that. But by the end of the Lambeth Conference in 2008, I concluded that so much of what had been said in recent years by some in the Church, particularly on the gay issue, was so moralistic and ungenerous that I did preach on the matter in Westminster Abbey.

I pointed out that our wider national society had, over a remarkably short period, fundamentally shifted its attitude towards gay relationships. According to British Social Trends, which is produced annually by the Office of National Statistics and is widely considered to be authoritative on social attitudes, in 1987 64 per cent of the population thought all homosexual acts were wrong. Twenty years later that had reduced to 18 per cent. That represented a massive shift in public attitudes over a very short period, and my guess was that many Christians were included in those who had made that change; I certainly had.

A careful examination of the very few biblical passages that appear to condemn homosexuality shows that what they were often condemning were not loving stable relationships between adults, but obviously unacceptable behaviour, such as homosexual rape in the story of Sodom and Gomorrah, or the widespread pederasty of Greek society condemned by Paul. No one wants to defend that. But many Christians would hold that biblical teaching must always be seen in the context of its age, and the responsibility now is to translate it into sensible practical moral teaching for today.

Some will nonetheless say that moral standards do not, and cannot change. But one significant and major change in church opinion about sexual behaviour happened in 1930, when the Lambeth Conference modified the very strong stance it had taken ten years earlier against any form of contraception. In 1920, the Lambeth bishops were utterly opposed to all forms of contraception and offered strong moral warnings against their use. By 1930 that had changed, and, much later, we even had the spectacle in the 1990s of the then Archbishop of Canterbury, George Carey, going to Rome to try to persuade the Pope to change his view on contraception. So much for unchanging moral principles!

It is significant to note that one of the Bishops opposed to the 1930s change, Charles Gore, a former Canon of the Abbey and by then Bishop of Oxford, opposed it on the grounds that he thought it would change the whole approach to sex if you allowed it to have a role in relationships independent of the possibility of procreation. The majority of Lambeth Bishops then did not mind making that change, and personally I am sure they were right; sex is not just about procreation but builds relationships. That change has implications for attitudes to homosexuality, for it does modify the whole question.

In that light, I read again the Bishops' statement on civil partnerships issued on 25 July 2005.[8] It is an extraordinary document. It says, rightly in my view, that 'marriage is a creation ordinance, a gift of God in creation and a means of his grace'. 'Marriage', it says, 'defined as a faithful, committed and permanent and legally sanctioned relationship between a man and a woman, is central to the stability and health of human society.' Amen to that. But it also says: 'Sexual intercourse, as an expression of faithful intimacy, properly belongs within marriage *exclusively*.' It seems from the British Social Trends report that 82 per cent of the population disagree in the case

8 House of Bishop's pastoral statement on Civil Partnerships, available on the Church of England website www.churchofengland.org.

of homosexuals, and that ought to make even the Bishops of an Established Church pause.

The Bishops' report also makes much of the fact that the government noted that the civil partnership legislation leaves 'entirely open the nature of the commitment that members of a couple choose to make to each other when forming a civil partnership. In particular, it is not predicated on the intention to engage in a sexual relationship.' This enabled the Bishops to say that 'it would not be right as a normal practice to encourage services of blessings for those entering civil partnerships', and it also allowed them to say of clergy entering such partnerships that 'it does not regard entering into a civil partnership as intrinsically incompatible with holy orders, provided the person concerned is willing to give assurances to his or her bishop that the relationship is consistent with the standards for the clergy set out in *Issues in Human Sexuality*', which presumably means that it should be a relationship in which sexual activity plays no part.

That seemed to me an extraordinarily convoluted way of approaching the matter. If some people are exclusively homosexual by orientation, and if they do not feel themselves to be called to celibacy, it must be healthier for them to live in a stable, publicly recognised relationship, and, if they want it, for that relationship to be acknowledged and blessed by the Church with honesty. Fidelity, rather than celibacy, should surely be what the Church encourages and advocates. In their 2005 statement, the Bishops appeared to be demanding that otherwise honourable and effective priests should lie. When I saw such emotional, intellectual and human dishonesty perpetrated in an episcopal document, I cannot say how pleased I was to work in the Abbey, in which no bishop has any authority whatsoever.

Since then Parliament has seen fit to allow marriage between people of the same sex. The official statement by the House of Bishops issued on 15 February 2014[9] about that change seemed on the one hand to offer a freedom to the laity to enter into same-sex marriages but on the other excluded clergy from following that path. That seems strange because some same-sex clergy couples I know demonstrate that their relationship is certainly one that is 'for the mutual society, help and comfort that the one ought to have of the other', and they model a good example of what marriage should be about. I also know some bishops are not happy with the present rules, and the Church has at least now committed itself to engaging in further full discussions on the matter. But some bishops enforce the still official line in ways that seem to me very destructive of the Church's standing among those many people who feel a basic tolerance of those who are different to themselves is a mark of decent society.

I do, of course, understand the difficulty of coping with change in one nation or group of nations for a body like the Anglican Communion spread across the world, where attitudes are very different in other countries. Maybe some form of tolerance between different bits of the communion is necessary, although not, I hope, tolerance of the persecution of those who are homosexual in orientation. The discussions initiated by the Church in both England but also in the wider Anglican Communion will no doubt be fraught and complex.

If being of homosexual orientation is not 'a sin', and I certainly understand those who are so orientated do not feel it to be so, then talk of forgiveness will seem demeaning. But sadly, and at least for the moment, there are churches within the Anglican Communion that do think it is. But if those from very

9 House of Bishops Statement available on the Liverpool Diocesan website: www.liverpool.anglican.org/House of Bishops/Statement on same sex marriages.

different cultures who do hold it to be 'a sin' can absorb that conviction within a greater commitment to forgiveness, which is far more fundamental to Christian teaching that anything on sex, that might provide a way forward.

I also wonder about what priority should be given by the Church of England to the needs of England. If we could become less obsessed by preserving the unity of the worldwide Church, and more concerned with what I believe the Church of England should be concerned about, serving the people of this basically tolerant nation, it would be to the good. It is a shift urgently needed.

For further reading

Forgiveness

James K. Voiss (2015) *Rethinking Christian Forgiveness.* Collegeville, MN: Liturgical Press.

Simon Wiesenthal (1998) *The Sunflower: On the Possibilities and Limits of Forgiveness.* New York: Schocken.

Interfaith engagement

Doctrine Commission of the Church of England (1995) *The Mystery of Salvation* London: Church House Publishing, Chapter 7 'Christ and World Faiths'.

John Hick (1974) *Truth and Dialogue; The Relationship between World Religions.* London: Sheldon Press, 1974.

Assisting those facing death

The parliamentary debates on assisted dying can be found on the parliamentary website parliament.uk/business/publications/hansard. The House of Lords debate was on 18 July 2014 and the Committee stage on 10 January 2015. The House of Commons debate was on 11 September 2015.

Human sexuality

The Report of the House of Bishops Working Group on Human Sexuality. 2013 Church House Publishing (The Pilling Report).

The House of Bishops set up this group under the chairmanship of Sir Joseph Pilling, and it recommended facilitated conversations within the Church of England and beyond, including on whether different rules for clergy and laity within the Christian Church were appropriate. It is available online at www.thechurchofengland.org/media/1891063/pillingreport.

11

FREEDOM OF THOUGHT IN THE CHURCH OF ENGLAND

The Church of England is a national church, open to anyone who wants to come. If it is being true to its character, it is generous in admitting people. Those who are baptised as infants have promises made on their behalf by godparents, which promises they can then make for themselves if they are confirmed. Those promises are of a rather general nature, and how they are interpreted is open to the individuals concerned. No layman or laywoman has even been prosecuted for heresy! The Bishops try to exercise some control over the clergy, but there is precious little they can do to the laity except sometimes, sadly, to ignore them.

What the Church of England has, in common with all other churches who assent to them, are the creeds, developed in the first few centuries of Christianity. Those creeds were often produced as a consequence of theological controversy and in many cases represented a compromise conclusion. I commented on their use in church services in Chapter 8. The notion that the Church has always believed the same thing throughout its history cannot be sustained by any careful examination of Church history. Even the apostles Paul and Peter disagreed about the quite fundamental issue of how to respond to Gentile converts to Christianity, so dispute within the Church is scarcely new.

In the case of the Church of England, the Thirty-Nine Articles of Religion, which were formulated in the sixteenth century in the context of the break from Rome, gave a fairly clear description of what Anglican clergy were supposed to believe then. However, by the middle of the nineteenth century there had been many occasions when their suitability for continued use in the Church was raised. A Parliamentary Bill of 1865 slightly weakened the official commitment of any clergyman, when it said only 'general assent' was required, although no definition of what that might mean was provided at the time. Since then in the second half of the nineteenth century and then throughout the twentieth century, the debates occasioned by the issues discussed in Chapter 2 have influenced how Anglican clergy have expressed their belief.

Within that context, then, what freedom do Anglican clergy have about what to believe? While much of the discussion about the theological issues themselves occurred in detailed academic publications by individual scholars, some more official statements issued on the authority of the Church of England could be laid alongside the more formal statements of belief contained in the creeds or Articles of Religion.

Of particular note was *Doctrine in the Church of England*, the report of the Commission on Christian Doctrine appointed by the Archbishops of Canterbury and York in 1922, but which was only finally published in 1938. For most of the Commission's life the Chairman was William Temple, Bishop of Manchester, then Archbishop of York and later Archbishop of Canterbury (1881–1944). The Commission allowed a wide range of different approaches to Scripture and matters of doctrine. In considering the existence of angels and demons, for example, it said language about them could be interpreted symbolically rather than literally.[1] On miracles, it recognised that science assumes regularities in nature, which made the notion of miraculous intervention difficult for many. It also recognised that:

> legends involving abnormal events have tended to grow very easily in regard to great religious leaders, and that in consequence it is impossible in the present state of knowledge to make the same evidential use of the narratives of miracles in the Gospels which appeared in the past.[2]

It allowed a similar range of views on such matters as the Virgin Birth and the Resurrection,[3] and when it came to the story of the Ascension it stated:

> Whatever may have been the nature of the event underlying those narratives, and whatever its relation to the Resurrection, its physical features are to be interpreted symbolically since they are closely related to the conception of heaven as a place locally fixed beyond the sky.'[4]

The report was welcomed by the Upper Houses (the Bishops) of the two official bodies of clergy in the Church of England at the time, the Convocations of Canterbury and York, who hoped that it would be widely studied 'in that spirit of open-minded devotion to truth and readiness to learn from every tradition of Christian thought which is characteristic of the report itself… while recognising the reality of the problems which scholars and theologians are handling and desiring to maintain the fullest

---

1 Doctrine Commission of the Church of England (1938) *Doctrine in the Church of England.* London: SPCK, p. 46 f.

2 Ibid. (1938) *Doctrine in the Church of England*, p.51.

3 Ibid. (1938) *Doctrine in the Church of England*, p.81 f. and p.83 f.

4 Ibid. (1938) *Doctrine in the Church of England*, p.89.

freedom of inquiry that is compatible with spiritual fellowship'.[5] There was wide press coverage of the report, and some disquiet about the breadth of interpretation allowed was expressed through a petition to the Upper Houses. The Bishops did not accept the more fundamental criticisms offered in that petition, but suggested an addition to their original motion saying that 'the Doctrine of the Church of England is now, as it has been in times past, the doctrine set forth in the Creeds, in the Prayer Book, and in the Articles of Religion'.[6] Sadly, the Second World War and its consequences stopped the widespread study that was recommended in the Convocation Resolutions, as the Church inevitably turned its attention to the more immediate matters raised by the war.

The next formal development came in the context of discussing the role of the Thirty-Nine Articles of Religion, developed in the Church of England just after the Reformation. In 1931, a Commission on the Staffing of the Parishes proposed that assent should no longer be required of clergy, but it was not until a report produced in 1968 on 'Subscription and Assent to the Thirty-Nine Articles' under the chairmanship of the then Bishop of Durham, Ian Ramsey (1915–72), that change actually happened.

It was noted that 'since the seventeenth century there have been those who have felt the demand for subscription tends to tyrannise the conscience in a way that destroys intellectual integrity'.[7] They believed that a wholesale revision of the Articles would be very difficult as some members of the Commission 'have very considerable doubts whether it would be possible to produce any single statement of reasonably short compass

5 Canterbury Chronicle of Convocation Proceedings for 1938, p.257 and 258.

6 York Journal of Convocation for the session on 2 and 3 June 1938, p.111.

7 1968 Report paragraph 17, p.16.

which could claim to define "the Christian faith" or even "the Anglican faith" along lines which would satisfy all Christians or all Anglicans'.[8] They were, however, also reluctant simply to abandon the Articles, so they proposed keeping them as part of the Anglican inheritance of faith without requiring specific subscription to them. The upshot of the whole discussion was the Preface to the Declaration of Assent that is now required of clergy, when the question asked is:

> The Church of England is part of the One, Holy, Catholic and Apostolic Church, worshipping the one true God, Father, Son and Holy Spirit. It professes the faith uniquely revealed in the Holy Scriptures and set forth in the catholic creeds, which faith the Church is called upon to proclaim afresh in each generation. Led by the Holy Spirit, it has borne witness to Christian truth in its historic formularies, the Thirty-Nine Articles of Religion, The Book of Common Prayer and the Ordering of Bishops, Priests and Deacons. In the declaration you are about to make, will you affirm your loyalty to this inheritance of faith as your inspiration and guidance under God in bringing the grace and truth of Christ to this generation and making Him known to those in your care?[9]

To which the priest or deacon gives his or her assent. Clearly, there was a major difference between giving specific or even general assent to the Thirty-Nine Articles and acknowledging them as part of the 'inheritance of faith' from which inspiration and guidance might be found in 'proclaiming the faith afresh in each generation'. It was and remains an effective way of acknowledging the past while giving some freedom for the future.

---

8 Ibid paragraph 85, p.44.

9 This can be found in *Common Worship: Services and Prayers for the Church of England.* London: Church House Publishing, 2000, p.xi.

Two reports of the Doctrine Commission, one entitled *Christian Believing* (1976) and one entitled *Believing in the Church* (1981), also opened up a wide range of theological debate with a semi-official imprimatur. The 1976 report identified different ways of responding to the Christian Faith found in the Church, ranging from those who found the creeds to be normative to those whose 'allegiance…is rather to the continuing Church of God than to any past beliefs and formulations, which they regard as inevitably relative to the culture of the age which produced them'.[10] They noted that there was a built-in conflict between those two ways of believing, and said:

> it is tempting in the weariness and distress of conflict between followers of a common Lord to opt for a radical and simplistic solution by which a decision is taken to rule out one or more of these competing attitudes. But we are convinced that any such decision would be disastrous for the health of the Church. The tension must be endured. What is important is that everything should be done (and suffered) to make it a creative tension – that is, not a state of non-communication between mutually embattled groups, but one of constant dialogue with consequent cross-fertilisation of ideas and insights.[11]

The later 1981 Report advocated the notion that belief was a corporate act by the whole Church in which different individuals might have an independent part to play. The report took the form of a series of essays by different members of the Commission. Canon Anthony Harvey, a former Canon of Westminster, wrote Chapter 11 'Markers and Signposts'. In it

10 Doctrine Commission of the Church of England (1976) *Christian Believing: The Nature of the Christian Faith and Its Expression in Holy Scripture and Creeds.* London: SPCK, p.37.

11 Doctrine Commission of the Church of England, *Christian Believing*, p.38.

he spoke of the effect of some recent controversial theological books and of the Commission's model of believing as a way of 'lessening that sense of threat and insecurity which are so often felt when traditional Christian beliefs are subject to radical questioning.'

He continued:

> When a bishop, or a Regius Professor of Divinity, or a group of distinguished theologians, publish interpretations of the Christian faith which seem to call into question doctrines whose truth is taken for granted by most church members, dismay is caused not only by the novelty of such thinking but by the apparent failure of the church authorities to make any clear response. *Honest to God*, *The Remaking of Christian Doctrine*, and *The Myth of God Incarnate* seemed to challenge the Church for a reply. But no official or authoritative reply was made...[12]
>
> These questions, and the dismay and insecurity they cause, are inevitable so long as the model with which we work is that of the individual believer having his faith supplied and monitored by the institutional organs of the Church. But they lose much of their menace if, as we have argued, the faith of both the Church and the individual is more accurately described as a kind of 'corporate believing', in which the individual, directly or indirectly, contributes to the formation of Church doctrine at the same time as the Church, through its worship, its ethos and its historic formularies, moulds the belief of the individual. The novel thinking of a radical theologian, or the explorations of small groups in the Church into new ways of formulating and expressing their Christian faith, can then be seen, not as a challenge to traditional doctrine which must at all costs be answered, but as a necessary stimulus to the kind of thinking

12 Doctrine Commission of the Church of England (1981) *Believing in the Church: The Corporate Nature of Faith.* London: SPCK, p.286.

> which must go on at all levels if the Church is to maintain a vigorous life.[13]

That did not prevent 15 years later others trying to institute more discipline on such matters among the clergy. In 1996 'Under Authority', a Report on Clergy Discipline dealt with how to respond to clergy who had clearly misbehaved in some way, but it also sought to include in the scope of its legislation discipline regarding doctrinal matters. At the time, I was a member of the General Synod, and I proposed an amendment suggesting that matters of doctrine and liturgy should be taken out of the legislation. Somewhat to my surprise, I was widely supported, and my amendment was carried. The Clergy Discipline Measure continued its course leading to the current procedures, which were undoubtedly needed, but doctrine and liturgy were omitted.

The bishops subsequently decided to set up a new body to consider doctrinal discipline, and I was among those asked to serve on the body. We met for nearly five years and finally produced a report that was considered by the General Synod in 2004. It recommended a procedure where, if enough people complained, a special tribunal would consider the case. There was unease in the Synod about how many complainants were needed to bring a case; most wanted a higher hurdle before any procedures were started. But there was also a wider unease about the whole process of setting up any tribunals that produced what the press would inevitably describe as 'heresy trials'. At the end of the debate the matter was put to a vote by houses, which meant that each of the three houses of the General Synod (Bishops, Clergy and Laity) had to approve the motion. It was defeated in the House of Clergy. As a member of the committee

13 Doctrine Commission, *Believing in the Church*, p.287.

who had produced the report, I thought I should vote in favour of it and did so, and was influenced by the comment of a liberal minded bishop whom I knew. I told him I was concerned about all sorts of people who held a particular view on what constituted orthodoxy going round the country searching for so-called heresy and initiating cases. He replied that he thought it would be good to have a system that could tell them they were wrong! However, I cannot say I was heartbroken at the final rejection of our proposals.

The result is that Anglican clergy are reasonably free to follow their own consciences in deciding how far to question traditional expressions of doctrine, and each person's contribution to those discussions becomes part of what the 1981 report called 'corporate believing'. That outcome should, however, be considered in the context of a remark made at some point during the course of the long debates on doctrinal discipline. An Australian sheep farmer was quoted as saying that on his farm he did not need fences, because at the centre of his farm there was a huge well and his sheep would not go too far from that. It is a good image for a confident and secure Church capable of accepting differences of interpretation amongst its members.

Conclusions

If pursuing truth wherever it might lead is a consequence of believing in God, as I argued in Chapter 3, then scepticism, far from being inimical to Christian Faith, is central to it. Any thoughtful Christian will want to examine what they believe and decide whether and how it is true or not. Sadly, though, except in the more trivial matters of life, truth is often not easy to arrive at. I am sure there will be some who read this book whose conclusions about what is true will be other than mine. They may be right! All I can say is what I believe to be true and why, and that is what I have tried to outline in this book. The search and at times the struggle to arrive at what might be true is all we can aim for, but wherever we feel we have found it then we have to live it. Whatever we believe to be true provides the story by which we live our lives.

For me, that means I am very content to describe myself as a Christian and to identify with the Christian Church, particularly in its Church of England form. A Church open to the world about it and ready to engage with it intellectually as well as ethically, and with the sort of freedom of interpretation about belief outlined in the last chapter, is one I am very happy to be a part of. I would, though, be happier if today it more openly and sympathetically engaged with the sources of scepticism I discussed in Chapter 2, and I hope this book might encourage that to happen. There is much to be gained by such open discussion and all that might be lost is a misplaced certainty, all too often buttressed by what I can only describe as Christian tribal defensiveness.

I suspect one of the issues that will cause some criticism of my stance is the historical scepticism I outline. I can only point out that it is not mine alone. The academic authorities I refer to were not way out radicals, but those who held major posts in highly reputable universities. Of course, in those universities there were others who took a different view. Such discussion is only healthy and right and I welcome the debate. What I dislike is simply ignoring the debates, yet sadly that is too often what I see in parts of the Church of England today.

The other matter that I suspect will disturb some is the suggestion from the world of neuroscience that ultimately all that we are is rooted in the material. Bentley Hart and John Hick disagree with that, as I said in Chapter 3, but as I explained ultimately what goes on in my mind passes through that material thing known as my brain, and when my brain dies then I believe my consciousness dies, as I said in Chapter 8. That is scarcely a new view; Baroness Mary Warnock, whom I quoted in that chapter, said it clearly in 2003, and I am sure others have said it, including some with religious faith. But it does represent a huge metaphysical shift from the language in which Christian faith was often couched in the past.

I was told when I was an undergraduate that the philosopher A.N. Whitehead once wrote that 'Christianity is a religion always searching for a metaphysic but never able to rest in one.'[1]That might be the context for one of the biggest challenges Christianity faces. If the metaphysical picture of human beings can no longer be of body, mind and spirit,

1 I have not been able to track down the basis of that quotation, but an internet search produces firstthings.com where an article 'Is there a Christian metaphysic?' includes the first part of the quotation.

but a psychosomatic unity where the body is essential for the mind, then much traditional Christian teaching will have to be modified. The Christian Church either has to show why that metaphysical change is untrue, or it has to adapt, possibly on the lines I argue in Chapter 7. Obviously, I believe such adaption is possible, but restating that question might be the legacy of this book.

Bibliography

Baelz, P. (1982) *Does God Answer Prayer?* London: Darton, Longman and Todd.

Baker, J.A. (1970) *The Foolishness of God.* London: Darton, Longman and Todd.

Baker, J.A. (1996) *The Faith of a Christian.* London: Darton, Longman and Todd.

Barbour, I. (2002) *Nature, Human Nature and God.* London: SPCK.

Caird, G.B. (1963) *St Luke.* Pelican New Testament Commentaries. London: Penguin.

Carnley, P. (1987) *The Structure of Resurrection Belief.* Oxford: Clarendon.

Carr, W. (1992) *Tested by the Cross.* London: Fount.

Davies, D. and Shaw, A. (1995) *Reusing Old Graves.* Crayford: Shaw and Son.

Doctrine Commission of the Church of England (1938) *Doctrine in the Church of England.* London: SPCK.

Doctrine Commission of the Church of England (1976) *Christian Believing: The Nature of the Christian Faith and Its Expression in Holy Scripture and Creeds.* London: SPCK.

Doctrine Commission of the Church of England (1981) *Believing in the Church: The Corporate Nature of Faith.* London: SPCK.

Doctrine Commission of the Church of England (1995) *The Mystery of Salvation.* London: Church House Publishing.

Dodd, C.H. (1936) *The Apostolic Teaching and its Developments.* London: Hodder and Stoughton.

Eliot, T.S. (1952) *The Complete Poems and Plays of T S Eliot.* London: Faber and Faber.

Farrer, A. (1964) *Saving Belief.* London: Hodder and Stoughton.

Farrer, A. (1966) *The Science of God.* London: Geoffrey Bles.

Farrer, A. (1967) *Faith and Speculation.* London: AandC Black.

Freud, S. (2008, first published in 1928) *The Future of an Illusion.* London: Penguin.

Greenberg, I. (2001) 'Cloud of Smoke Pillar of Fire. Judaism, Christianity and Modernity after the Holocaust.' In Michael Morgan (ed.) *A Holocaust Reader.* Oxford: Oxford University Press, pp. 102–14.

Hart, D.B. (2013) *The Experience of God: Being, Consciousness, Bliss.* London: Yale University Press.

Hastings, A. (2000) 'Jesus.' In A. Hastings *et al.* (eds.) *Oxford Companion to Christian Thought.* Oxford: Oxford University Press, pp. 340–2 and 640.

Hick, J. (1974) *Truth and Dialogue: The Relationship Between World Religions.* London: Sheldon Press.

Hick, J. (ed.) (1977) *The Myth of God Incarnate.* London: SCM Press.

Hick, J. (2010) *The New Frontier of Religion and Science.* Basingstoke: Palgrave Macmillan.

Hillesum, E. (1999) *An Interrupted Life: The Diaries and Letters of Etty Hillesum 1941–1943.* London: Persephone Books.

Houlden, J.L. (1992) *Jesus: A Question of Identity.* London: SPCK.

James, W. (1977, first published in 1902) *The Varieties of Religious Experience.* London: Fount Paperback.

Jung, C.G. (1961, first published in 1933) *Modern Man in Search of a Soul.* London: Routledge and Keegan Paul.

Knox, J. (1967) *The Humanity and Divinity of Christ.* Cambridge: Cambridge University Press.

Küng, H. (1978) *On Being a Christian.* Glasgow: Collins Fount Paperback.

Lampe, G. (1977) *God as Spirit: The 1976 Bampton Lectures.* London: SCM Press.

Marsh, H. (2014) *Do No Harm. Stories of Life, Death and Brain Surgery.* London: Weidenfeld and Nicholson.

Mooney, B. (ed.) (2003) *Devout Sceptics: Conversations on Faith and Doubt.* London: Hodder and Stoughton.

Nineham, D. (1977) 'Epilogue' in John Hick (ed.), *The Myth of God Incarnate.* London: SCM Press.

Peacock, A. (2000) 'Science and the Future of Theology: Critical Issues.' *Zygon 35*, pp. 119–40.

Phillips, J.B. (1965) *Your God is Too Small.* London: Wyvern Books.

Polkinghorne, J. (1996) *Scientists as Theologians.* London: SPCK.

Purcell, W. (ed.) (1966) *The Resurrection: A Discussion Arising from Broadcasts by G W H Lampe and D M Mackinnon.* London: Mowbray.

Rees, M. (2002) *Our Cosmic Habitat.* London: Weidenfeld and Nicholson.

Richards, H.J. (1973) *The First Christmas: What Really Happened?* London: Mowbray.

Richards, H.J. (1975) *The Miracles of Jesus: What Really Happened?* London: Mowbray.

Richards, H.J. (1980) *The First Easter: What Really Happened?* Glasgow: Collins Fount Paperbacks.

Robinson, J.A.T. (1960) *Liturgy Coming to Life.* London: Mowbray and Co.

Robinson, J.A.T. (1963) *Honest to God.* London: SCM Press.

Sacks, J. (2003) *The Dignity of Difference.* London: Continuum.

Sacks, J. (2011) *The Great Partnership: God, Science and the Search for Meaning.* London: Hodder and Stoughton.

Studdert Kennedy, G.A. (2006) *The Unutterable Beauty: The Collected Poetry of G.A. Studdert Kennedy.* Liskeard: Diggory Press.

Temple, F. (1884) *The Relations between Religion and Science: Eight Lectures Preached Before the University of Oxford in the Year 1884.* London: Macmillan.

Theissen, G. (1987) *The Shadow of the Galilean.* London: SCM.

Tillich, P. (1962) *The Shaking of the Foundations.* London: Pelican Books.

Vermes, G. (2000) *The Changing Faces of Jesus.* London: Penguin.

Voiss, J.K. (2015) *Rethinking Christian Forgiveness.* Collegeville, MN: Liturgical Press.

Ward, K. (2004) *What the Bible Really Teaches: A Challenge for Fundamentalists.* London: SPCK.

White, S. (2012) *Jesus and the Christ.* Dublin: The Columba Press.

White, V. (2006) *Life Beyond Death*. London: Darton, Longman and Todd.

Wiesel, E. (1996) *All Rivers Run in the Sea: Memoirs*. London: Harper Collins.

Wiesel, E. (2006) *Night*. London: Penguin.

Wiesenthal, S. (1998) *The Sunflower: On the Possibilities and Limits of Forgiveness*. New York: Schocken.

Wiles, M. (1974) *The Remaking of Christian Doctrine*. London: SCM Press.

Wiles, M. (1977) 'Christianity without Incarnation?' in John Hick (ed.), *The Myth of God Incarnate*. London: SCM Press, pp.1–13.

Wiles, M. (1986) *God's Action in the World: The Bampton Lectures for 1986*. London: SCM Press.

Wiles, M. (1999) *Reason to Believe*. London: SCM Press.

Williams, H. (1965) *The True Wilderness*. London: Constable.

Williams, R. (2014) *Meeting God in Mark*. London: SPCK.

Wright, N.T. (2003) *The Resurrection of the Son of God*. London: SPCK.

Index